MEET ME BY THE RIVER

A Woman's Healing Journey

Ilene Aliyah Alexander

© 2014
Three Dashes Publications

"As a hospice chaplain and grief counselor, I have heard countless stories... many involve sorrow and loss... but never have I been so impressed as when I met Aliyah... She knows how to listen to her heart... and has turned *tragedy into joy*... She wrote much of this book while being able to move only her wrist!"
- Rev. Terri Daniel: Author, Educator, End-of-Life Advisor, Interfaith Chaplaincy.

"Aliyah lives a new vision of healing... one where our 'curriculums' are our steppingstones... and our common ground to grow and expand a more loving world."
- Judith Oakland: MA and Licensed Professional Counselor.

"Aliyah's blog truly puts life in perspective and serves as a reminder of how the human spirit can triumph... Through her intimate reflections of her transformative life, she's offered me a priceless gift... the reminder that even in the face of seemingly bleak outcomes, I am exactly where I need to be... and I say a prayer of thanks. "
- Lynne Kaplan: Photographer

"I am continually nourished and inspired by the clarity and courage with which Aliyah writes about inner and inter-relatedness, the shadow, suffering, joy and the liberation of being with what *Is*... Her voice transmits directly to my heart..." - Kathryn Brady - Author

"An inspiring chronicle of a heroine's journey towards ever deepening love!" - Allison Wonderland- artist

"Aliyah's honest sharing of her life encourages us all to step up and take a look into the dark places of our own lives."
- Sage Brown: Saguache County School Board President

ACKNOWLEDGEMENTS

First I want to thank my inner circle over the past two decades, without which this book would never have been born... I want to thank Anna, my original champion... Alex, Diana and Kathryn for endless inspiration and support... I want to thank Lynne, who not only brought my story to life through her photography, but also climbed on an elephant with me in Jaipur, India... To Judith who deeply supports and loves like a Sister... And to all the women who literally have my back on a daily basis: Allison, Matney, Lauren, Leah and Lauren K... To the two men who support my physical well-being and my heart... Harald and Bruce... To my 'nonviolent' sisters, Sage, Kirsten, Gussie, Sophia and JoAnne.

I also wish to thank my dear former colleague and friend Janie Jane who asked me decades ago at my lowest point... "if this plays out, how are you going to live your life?"

To my parents, brothers, cousins and their immediate families, thank you for forming and informing who I am.

I thank my children Casey and Jordan for pushing me to live a life with the greatest integrity and courage and Kumar who joined our family later and brought much love... You all have taught me to love like I never had before.

I thank my grandsons River and Luc who bring me more joy than I ever imagined possible. To future family members, I will Know and love you.

You may reach Aliyah at www.meetmebytheriver.net

Thanks to Lynne Kaplan for the wonderful art included in this book.

Lynne Kaplan is a natural light photographer, and currently Associate Director for the international Miami Street Photography Festival. Seeing the world through a lens encourages her to reflect on the artistry and poetry of even the most mundane places and everyday experience. It's her way of stopping to smell the roses.
You can find Lynne at www.lynnellenphotography.com and http://turningart.com/artists/artist-lynne-kaplan

Christopher Kaufman
Editor, Layout and
Director of --- Publications

© 2014
Three Dashes Publications

ALL RIGHTS RESERVED

TABLE OF CONTENTS

Foreword
Introduction — 1

Chapter One: The Labyrinth of Illness: From Tragedy to Transcendence — 4
Shattered — 5
The Hybridization of Aliyah — 7
New Delhi, India, July — 12
New Delhi, India, November — 15
Creeping Beauty — 18
Facing the Family Pathology — 20

Chapter Two: Bridge Across Forever — 23
My Animal Clan — 24
The Lie Underneath the Illness — 30
POEM - *Four Elements* — 33
The Genesis — 34
Uncle — 38
Liberation — 40
My Father's Greatest Teaching — 42
Across the Bridge of Hope — 46
Pass the Prune Juice, Dammit — 50
Mama Mia — 53
POEM - *The arms are falling* — 55

Chapter Three: The Great Purifier — 58
Integration of the Feminine: The Keystone — 59
A Brazilian Mystery — 61
The Asklepian Game — 63
Co-Madre Honor: The Sacred Triangle — 67
Harald and Bonnie Got It Going On — 70
Katrina: The Great Purifier — 74
POEM - *Years in the trenches* — 78

Chapter Four: It Aint Over Til It's Over   79
Initiations Into Diversity and Reconciliation   80
POEM - *Alone again*   85
What Evokes Hope for Humanity in You?   86
Mr. Magoo and Other Spiritual Teachers   89
Truth or Symbolic Story: Healing Beyond Lifetimes   91
Civilization: The Development of Compassion   96
Redemption: Shawshank Style   101
It Ain't Over Til It's Over   105

Chapter Five: The Vicissitudes of Healing   110
Moving Forward   111
What Do You Need Awchie?   114
Ascendance: Working with Soul Themes   117
POEM - *Caught in the Magnetic field...*   121
The Metaphor of Social Media   122
Meta-Morphing Intransigent Beliefs   125
Rebecca   128
The Vicissitudes of Healing   131
Transmutation of Violence: A Personal Journey   136

Chapter Six: Dancing with the Devil   140
The Tao of Kenny   141
Suicide is Painless, It Brings On many Changes   143
Caregiving Part 1: A Holographic Paradigm   147
Dancing with the Devil   151
The Path of the Wounded Healer   157
Encountering Shadow: A Risky Personal Disclosure   162
Springtime in the Rockies   166

Chapter Seven: Taking the Leap   168
Generational Healing Through the Ritual of Birth   169
POEM - *Falling into myself*   174
Leading from Vulnerability: A Paradigm Shift   175

Let Go, Let God: Walking My Talk	179
My Green Light is On Or The Tao of Kenny Revisited	183
The Body as Messenger	187
One Prerequisite for a Call to Service	190
POEM - *The Substance*	192
Roots of Love Through Generations	193
Don't Just Do Something, Sit There	198
POEM - *Take The Leap*	200

Chapter Eight: The Canary in the Coal Mine — 201

Life in the Holy	202
An Optimistic Retrospective	205
Getting Thrown, Sometimes	208
Experimental Psychology Revisited: Healing the Sacred Feminine-Part 1	210
Experimental Psychology Revisited: Healing the Sacred Feminine-Part 2	213
POEM - *Your love comes to me...*	216
Shut-In, Bedridden, Housebound... Oh My!	217
Transparency: A Gift or a Curse	221
Caregiving Part 2: A Holographic Paradigm	224
Our Interracial Gospel Choir	228
The Canary in the Coal Mine	229

Chapter Nine: I Will Meet You By The River — 231

Illness: A Transpersonal Perspective	232
Triangles: The Power of Three	236
River and Luc	240
Caregiving: Transcending Duality	242
POEM - *The waxing and waning of emotion*	244
I Wouldn't Want To Be a Member Of a Group That Would Have Me As a Member - Groucho Marx	245
I Will Meet You By The River	247
Final Meditation	249

FOREWORD

- Rev. Terri Daniel: ordained interfaith minister, clinical chaplain and end-of-life educator.

As a hospice chaplain and grief counselor, I have heard countless stories of sorrow and loss, and I've watched people respond to those losses in ways that span the spectrum from anger and vindictiveness to grace and gratitude.

Aliyah Alexander has grieved many losses in addition to the loss of her physical functionality and the productive life she lived before being stricken with Multiple Sclerosis (MS). In the pages of this book, she takes grace and gratitude to a whole new level by showing us that living with a degenerative, life-threatening illness can be seen as a spiritual gift rather than a bitter defeat.

She is a natural-born healer who spent most of her life helping others. A survivor of childhood sexual abuse, she earned a Master's degree in social work from Tulane University, and spent ten years working with at-risk children. She was in the honor society for pre-med, but opted to study alternative modalities instead, and became a facilitator of healing breath work under the tutelage of the legendary Stanislav Grof. She was also an accomplished athlete...a swimmer, a racquetball tournament player and an equestrian who galloped across the desert in front of the Egyptian pyramids.

Her professional resume is impressive, but her spiritual resume is even more remarkable. She wrote this book using only her wrist, which she uses to control her dictation software, and using that same software, she facilitates an online women's therapy group. She cannot move any part of her body other than the one wrist, and at this writing, she is losing her ability to swallow and process food. Her physical therapist told her that she was the most disabled person he had ever seen living alone.

I first met Aliyah when she called me for phone counseling in 2010. Her MS was progressing rapidly, and she was wondering whether to stay in Pennsylvania where family members could help with her care, or move back to her beloved home in the magical town of Crestone, Colorado, a high desert haven in the Sangre de Cristo Mountains. If Aliyah knows anything, she knows how to listen to her heart, and she knew that true spiritual healing would happen in Crestone. She returned to the mountains, and now lives there alone, where, with the help of part-time caregivers, she spends her time meditating, writing, using various curative protocols, and following a daily routine that includes spending one hour in a standing frame and 20 minutes in the sun for "photon therapy."

Aliyah knows that it's not just about healing the physical body, but about connecting with the soul on much larger playing field in which the body serves a specific spiritual purpose. Aliyah's body is teaching her one the most powerful lessons in human experience…how to transcend ego by releasing attachment to the body's form. A soul who chooses this path is making the highest possible commitment to spiritual awakening.

In Aliyah's words, "The greatest impulse in dealing with this progressive autoimmune illness is to stop, rest and wait for energy." In a medical sense, this is good advice, but as a spiritual metaphor it is an important directive. We can all stop, rest and wait for energy if we trust in our inner guidance and allow ourselves to be still and listen.

Aliyah is an expert at that.

INTRODUCTION

Years ago, in my most desperate moments, the writings I call Songs From The Labyrinth were born. They took the form of an ongoing blog. I am happy to share them with you in this new book.

I hope my journey helps you in yours.

Throughout my life I had been a very athletic person. I competed in sports such as swimming, horseback riding and racquet sports, just to name a few. If I could rely on anything, it was my physicality.

But as my body began to weaken I have been forced to face my greatest fear, *that I was alone in the universe and helpless.* In our society fear is an emotion that is demonized. Fear begets fear and that was certainly true for me.

New Age theories were being disseminated that distorted Truths and had the effect of blaming the individual experiencing the illness.

I felt desperate as my body began to break down, desperate to find affirmation that this experience might be regenerative, that it could be a door opening to fulfill my deepest heart's desire *to do what I came here to do.*

I consulted libraries of books and there was nothing to allay my fears. I went from person to person and to every healer and healing protocol I could find to support my body.

I felt that to redeem myself spiritually my body needed to heal. When I saw that my body was continuing to weaken, I realized that there was nothing to be found external to myself and that I had to look inward for my truth *and this is where my spiritual journey really begins.*

I have been a willful person my whole life. This illness, one of the most progressive forms of MS, brought me into the depths of my darkness. During my most despair filled moments my inner voice became louder and stronger, and that has been the paradox.

As a competitive athlete with many blue ribbons I never felt powerful, but as a virtual quadriplegic I know that I am a powerhouse!

This quality became integrated into my identity. Instead of seeing myself as weak I came to know that I am courageous, courageous to take on my fear, to survive *and find joy in the experience.*

I could fulfill my greatest yearnings, connect with my desires to evolve spiritually, to be of service to others and *to help them find self-love.* I learned that when an individual goes through a catastrophic event there is the opportunity for tremendous growth and spiritual evolution.

I learned that anyone struggling with catastrophic injuries or illnesses can find hope, that they can be courageous to take on such extreme circumstances *and know that transcendence is possible.*

There are times when fear and loneliness can be consuming, times when medical science is grossly inadequate and times when friends are incapable of sharing the experience.

It is important to know that many people understand and will have compassion. Everyone is facing challenges on some level. I have learned early on not to compare my circumstances with others. *Empathy is the elixir for everyone facing challenges.*

At my darkest moment I began these writings. Sharing them with you is part of my journey.

I hope my journey helps you in yours.

With hope,

- Aliyah

CHAPTER ONE

The Labyrinth of Illness : From Tragedy to Transcendence

"A hero leaves her comfortable surroundings to venture into a challenging, unfamiliar world..." Joseph Campbell

SHATTERED

Blog Entry : April 22, 2012

"Shattered, like a windowpane... Something deep inside of me is shattered..." – Linda Ronstadt

It was early 2007. We were moving to Crestone, a small city in south-central Colorado, to be near the place where I'd previously gone camping and enjoyed nature. David, my husband at the time drove as I sat and enjoyed the shifting countryside. The horses were shipped separately, thank goodness and the horse trailer was filled with our artwork. At one point we were parked at the side of the road, my wheelchair went down a hill and I shattered my femur. *Why are my transitions wrought with so many complications?*

Having calamities while I'm on the precipice of something new is a recurring pattern, a pattern that represents an imprint from earlier in my life - the kind of thing that can be worked with when brought to consciousness. It is significant is that this happened with a caregiver present and even participating in the calamity.

I've come to believe that with chronic illness and life altering accidents, there may be an unconscious expression that can lead to a form of healing. Contrary to much of the new age pop psychology theories, sometimes an illness or an accident can lead to a deeper level of healing...*that the soul desires.*

Stephen Levine, who worked for many years with Elisabeth Kübler-Ross in the field of death and dying, in his book *Healing Into Life and Death* writes that many of the people he has worked with who are dealing with illness have found a cure, and that the person with the cure can be so difficult that they often alienate the people around them. He has also seen situations where the person heals, the heart comes to completion and the body dies. Perhaps the vehicle is no longer necessary once the healing has occurred.

I believe that our past life Karma becomes 'imprinted' during our birth process and is a manifestation of what we have come here to work on. This concept of 'birth-process imprinting' may seem far-fetched to some, but I've experienced it over and over again and have the stitches and casts to prove it. I'd like to note that this concept comes from a theory from one of my mentors, Stanislav Grof, M.D. PhD, in his work with *Holotropic breathwork*.

THE HYBRIDIZATION OF ALIYAH

Blog Entry : April 22, 2012

"We dance alone. We dance together. We dance each other into rhythm." – Anonymous

It was ironic. Just as I was finding my footing as a psychotherapist, my very foundation began to quake. I started sorting out attachment issues, grief issues, sexual abuse issues…and the unraveling began.

My course of study made my curiosity and intention to make sense of *My Story* that much more pressing.

BACKSTORY

In my late twenties, while blessed with my wonderful daughter Casey, I was in a very difficult marriage. My former roommate, Lucetta, strongly urged me, in fact begged me to see a therapist. I think she just couldn't stand to hear me complain about my husband for one more minute.!

So after interviewing many therapists, I joined an intensive psychotherapy group. I attended this group at least three times a week and participated in intensives on the beach in Florida which lasted five-days at a clip.

I developed strong bonds with this new family, so strong that to this day, almost thirty-five years later I am still close friends with three of the women I met at that time - friends that I still communicate with on a daily basis!

For many years, this community was *my family* and I believe this experience gave me the foundation that my professional self needed.

I was no longer the nubile person who entered the Tulane University graduate program. I had explored every facet that was accessible to my conscious mind and much that was unconscious. The act of seeing other people do their own inner exploration was synergistic and it was significant that for the first time in my life I felt no depression.

This community ended when the facilitator moved to Lake Tahoe. Nevertheless, my internal journey had begun in a big way and would continue for the rest of my life.

'MY GURU'

In 1985, my second husband began therapy with a psychiatrist in New Orleans who gave up his psychiatric license to become a guru!

Do I hear the word 'unconventional'? Yes, John's work was unusual, but in all fairness the community we developed was composed of doctors and lawyers and artists. None of us were slouches and John was quite brilliant and gifted, aside from his eccentricities.

This work was my initiation beyond the parameters of ego. This is where my path diverged from past associations and my work on a spiritual level began to *accelerate*. I just tried to hold on to my hat and even that was hard to do much of the time!

In the past, when I had joined the group psychotherapy community in my twenties, I was an agnostic/atheist. Being totally pragmatic...*God just didn't make sense.*

But now, during my work with John, I had my first direct experience with God. From the beginning there were issues that John and I disagreed about. I was raised Jewish where there is an emphasis on exclusivity and I disagreed with it even then, I could not subscribe to excluding others - whereas John demanded exclusivity. So, contrary to his teaching, for me there was not just *one way*. I knew this in my soul and during those few years with him he prophesied that I would leave him because of this issue...*He was right.*

My next unconventional teacher was an older German woman in Taos, New Mexico, *Mathilde*. She facilitated a form of breathwork that she'd developed after studying under Stanislav Grof.

I had done much of my ego and emotional work, then my spiritual work, now I was putting it all together. I was drilling down into the depths of my unconscious to find the pieces I had disowned, feared or clearly did not yet have the resources to address. This is also known as shadow work.

The physical symptoms of MS had started a year or two before working with this new teacher, so my pump was primed. I was willing to discover what needed to be uncovered and loved. There was a whole community that formed around this breathwork as well.

ALIYAH

Around this time I went to a heart retreat in Galesteo, New Mexico. There were two women named Ilene, myself being one of them. The practitioners asked if one of us had a spiritual name and for years I had been called *Aliyah* (AHliyah) in my spiritual community, so I claimed it.

Aliyah is a Hebrew word that means to ascend, or to go to Jerusalem (which is on a mountain, so you must ascend). My new name stuck in my spiritual community and *Aliyah* was born.

At my third wedding in 2003, one of the three women friends I had made during my first therapy experience stood up and declared, *"I have known Ilene for over twenty years and her life has always been about transformation."*

Whether I came to life primed for this spiritual work or I was led to it, *the work has changed me.* I can no longer relate to the person that I was.

There have been very few people who could maintain an intimate connection with me through all these changes. Other than family, there has been one friend from my home town of Scranton who has maintained a connection. Diane moved with her family to Jerusalem and perhaps that and our deep connection have made the difference. I believe that is the natural order of things. There is grief for the old life, there is no denying that. However once the genie is out of the bottle there is no going back.

HEALING IN INDIA

I believe we are all pilgrims and whatever challenge we take on to accelerate the journey is a sacred mission.

My symptoms began very subtly in the late 1980s. I had increasing anxiety, which was a kind of fearful intuition that I had a neurological illness. I went to many doctors over the ensuing fifteen years and accelerated my body, mind and spirit work. In 2003, while in Ireland on tour with my gospel choir, I began to limp. The doctor finally agreed to an MRI...*That led to my MS diagnosis.*

In 2004 I received a Lyme disease diagnosis. The last tick bite I had was in the late 1990s. It is controversial whether Lyme disease leads to MS, Parkinson's, ALS, and others, but I believe that it can. I underwent Lyme disease treatment for many years without relief. Many of my friends with Lyme disease improved greatly. Some forms are harder to treat, I guess I am in this category.

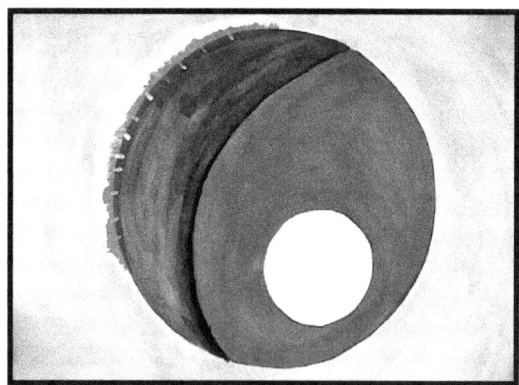

Breathwork Mandala, Arroyo Secco - 1995

NEW DELHI, INDIA, JULY 2010

Blog Entry : April 23, 2012

After following the Lyme disease protocol for years with no improvement, I read about some lyme disease patients having success with embryonic stem cells in India.

Due to the political climate, the United States was way behind in research. Even in India the treatment was controversial, even so far as to include the doctor who developed the process. In my opinion, the medical establishment is closed to areas that are not controlled by pharmaceutical companies.

The main controversy is in the use of an embryo. The doctor in India was a fertility specialist who had an embryo donated from a couple who were going to discard it. This embryo was processed in such a way that multiple cells were harvested and used on over a thousand patients. I heard a story in the hospital that the process somehow involved an accident in the laboratory, but it is my belief that there...*are no accidents.*

In 2010, after careful research, I wrote a letter requesting treatment at the hospital in India. I spoke to a few patients who had gone there for treatment. I believe that after attempting so many different areas of healing and finding little to no progress, I was clearly bumping into something that was blocking my healing on the level of the unconscious.

I felt that if I were going to find whatever was in the way of my healing, that India would be the place to enjoin this quest.

MOTHER INDIA

As I prepared for the two-month trip, I began experiencing vertigo for the first time. When I feel fear my body goes haywire.

Nevertheless, I pushed through and got to the hospital in India! During my first night there in a meditation, I saw an Indian man and a woman in a sari. I thought they were doctors, but I realized that they were the parents of the embryo. It was clear that they supported the process!

During the first two days, I was sent to other hospitals for diagnostic baseline studies. The results were reviewed with the doctors, and I knew where I stood. The lesions were all through my brain and thick on the cervical and lumbar areas of the spine.

On the night of my second day in India I received my first injection of stem cells. With each injection I felt an increase in anxiety. The infusion of life force seem to be bumping up against something very dense and amorphous. I was unable to eat, unable to sleep and everywhere I went I carried a bag to throw up in.

During the second week of an eight-week stay, after a fitful night of insomnia, I had a *'Peak Experience'* which concerned my son Jordan.

Jordan and his father, my second husband Sid, had many parallel experiences in their lives. Sid once told me that watching Jordan grow up felt like he was looking in a mirror. I remembered that Sid's mother had died tragically when he was in his twenties and saw the parallel with Jordan's experience. I saw the trajectory of the storyline and realized that I did not have to play it out!

There was an existential shift...*I no longer felt anxiety or fear.* I knew that breaking this script was essential, **feelings of liberation replaced** my anxiety.

During the remaining weeks in India, my strength and range increased as well as my dexterity. I began wheeling myself from physiotherapy to my room, which I hadn't been able to do for years. The atrophy in my arms began filling out and I was showing off my biceps on Skype sessions with my children. My son remarked, *"Whoa mom, put those guns away!"*

At the end of the eight weeks, I repeated the scans and found much improved blood circulation in my brain and the MRIs now showed lesions around C5 and the lumbar area only. My brain was clear and the vertigo was gone. The doctor told me that this was *the most improved MRI he had seen of someone with MS.*

Interestingly enough, when I returned to the states and I told many different doctors about the experience, they were totally uninterested in seeing the scans...*People are not comfortable shifting paradigms.* When I see what I went through, why would I expect that they would be any different?

NEW DELHI, INDIA, NOVEMBER 2010

Blog Entry : April 24, 2012

"Resurrection means the opening of the inner eye, to see that there is no death." - Marianne Williamson

After I returned to the US in July, 2010, I continued to improve. I could take my clothes off by myself and I continued to strengthen and I attended my daughter's wedding.

It had been my hope and prayer to have more strength for that blessed event, and it was everything had I hoped for and more.

Ironically, the ceremony was half Hindi and half Jewish, which seemed very fitting now that *I had Indian stem cells!*

And, true to Indian tradition, not only were my daughter and her new husband united but the two families were as well. I had experienced another Indian tradition from the inside out.

With a degenerative illness, one has to return to India every three months to stop the progression and reverse the illness. Especially with Lyme disease, it is important to stop the infection from mobilizing the immune system. I was scheduled to return in November. My core was beginning to weaken again, and I was ready.

But something very strange happened when I was packing to leave. Usually when I was packing for a trip, my great dane, Basha, would jump in the car. When she wasn't coming with us, we had to be sure to keep the doors closed while getting ready. This ritual had been going on for years. However, this time when I was packing, she slept.

When I got in the car, I looked at her and, instead of trying to join me, she walked next door with a sense of resignation. In retrospect, I realize that there was something else going on, outside of my awareness.

My girlfriend, Lynne, from college accompanied me on this trip to India. She and I had many adventures through the years, and now she'd chosen to take a month out of her life and support me on my journey.

That is an enormous amount of love to give, as well as to receive, and I'll never forget it. We went to India together and I was open and ready for more improvement! What seems to be consistent in life is that I never know which way the winds will blow.

When in India, I got an e-mail about my precious, beloved Basha. She was not eating and we wondered if it had to do with me being gone. Then I received an e-mail that she was going to the veterinarian and she needed emergency surgery for a uterine infection. I sat up all night with my computer on my lap while she went into surgery. After many hours of waiting, I got the word that she never recovered.

Basha had not just been a pet, she was a *'service dog'*. The connection between a disabled person and their service dog is incomparable. The mixture of feelings that welled up in me was extreme. My body shut down and the grief could be felt within ten feet of my body. The medical staff worked with me as best they could. I could it see on their face, *"don't do this"* they seemed to say.

I didn't know how not to. It is still extremely difficult, I started another post on my beloved dog a few weeks ago but I've been avoiding it.

I know, like everything excruciating in life, there will be a resulting experience of liberation. And that is precisely what happened. I developed a lung infection so severe that I was on constant antibiotics and nebulizer treatments for the rest of my stay in India, though I did manage to go to the Taj Mahal and to Jaipur to ride an elephant!

Unlike my first trip to India, I did not experience any physical improvement, but the way I see it, the stem cells helped me stay in my body long enough to release my best friend into Spirit.

CREEPING BEAUTY

Blog Entry : April 26, 2012

As I grew up, I was told that I was very pretty. This seemed odd to me because my internal experience was not consistent with what other people saw. I eventually learned to accept people's reactions, kind of how one might receive a collective hallucination. *When is it that the self-hatred begins?*

Does it start before the age of three? What two-year-old child has an investment in how others perceive her?

There's a 'game' people play, which Eric Berne - the Canadian born psychiatrist best known as the creator of 'transactional analysis' - called 'Creeping Beauty'. His description of 'Creeping Beauty' details the emotional predicament a woman can find herself in as she ages and desperately tries hold on to her disappearing youth and beauty.

I remember feeling that I was at risk, that I was attached to my external appearance and I wanted to be careful to avoid the 'Creeping Beauty' pitfall.

I think the men in my family had an attachment to women being beautiful. It's interesting that at three years old I would feel the pressure. Over the years I came to learn that my true attractiveness to other people had nothing to do with my outer appearance...*this knowledge was hard won.*

In college, after a very disappointing relationship, I gained forty pounds. I began to understand that extra weight was like armoring, protection against what felt unsafe.

It wasn't until my forties that I realized that what truly draws people is what my teachers referred to as my *'Light'*. This is a quality that everybody has, but I bet 'Creeping Beauties' never get to find this out!

The women in my lineage have carried a great deal of unexamined self-hatred. A history of forebears 'Raped by Cossacks' didn't help, if you'll forgive a reference to Woody Allen's Annie Hall.

During the time of pogroms and concentration camps, the oppressors didn't discriminate between genders. The way I think about it, the experiences of my ancestors paved the way for me to do the self exploration necessary to increase my quality of life. Because of them...*survival was handled*. My children and I could now create our lives using what we've been given.

FACING THE FAMILY PATHOLOGY

Blog Entry : April 29, 2012

"Grief can open the door to everlasting love." – Tara Brach

The last time I went snow skiing was in Colorado with my former stepson. It was the year 2005. I was on skis and he on his snowboard. We must have made over thirty runs up the mountain.

As always, it was a euphoric experience for me and reminded me of my childhood, where I skied weekly with my high school classmates. This time however, there was a compulsive nature to my skiing, almost as if I knew I had to get all the skiing in today for the rest of my life.

At the time, I wasn't aware that this 'premonition' was driving the experience, but this was the last time I snow skied. In the past, when I wasn't snow skiing I was water skiing. When I wasn't snow or water skiing I was riding horses. When I wasn't doing sports, I was renovating buildings or creating my garden.

When Eric, my first husband and I got together, we renovated buildings. We demolished a two-story camelback in an historic area of New Orleans with a hammer and crowbar. I remember single handedly pushing an old sofa out of the second-story window with Eric cheering me on.

Later on, when David and I got together, he lived in a camp with no running water on a cypress swamp with Spanish moss everywhere. We quietly paddled in a pirogue (Cajun canoe) tracker-style looking for wildlife. We swam in the swamp, hiked for many miles and camped out for weeks at a time in the mountains. So you see, my previous life was inextricably interwoven with being physically active and constantly in nature.

Professionally, I worked at a community mental health center for forty hours a week specializing in children, their families, and women's issues. I carried a pager after hours for emergency evaluations. Many of my contacts were people who had just attempted suicide or were metaphorically on 'the ledge' and needed to be talked down. These were my favorite evaluations because people this desperate were, ironically, *also open to change.* I found it easy to give them a sense of 'the bigger picture' at a time when they most needed it.

I passed my boards and started my private practice. I was able to stop doing the emergency after hours evaluations which had left me sleep deprived. Nevertheless, I had a full professional schedule. On top of all this, I raised my children as a single mom. My son gave me a mug as a present for workaholics that read, *"Thank God it's Monday!"*

He was able to use humor, but he clearly felt frustrated that I was so busy all the time. He told me straight, *"I want to spend more time with you."*

 Being torn between this level of activity and the desires of my son, I began to look at what was driving this excessive behavior. What was I running from?

The more I worked, the more desperate I became to stay in motion. The greater the desperation, the more determined I was to understand this behavior. I knew it was multigenerational. My family is replete with addictive behaviors, from workaholism, anger addiction and prescription drug use to the misuse of food and alcohol for self soothing. Both of my brothers are in recovery for addictions. I finally built up enough courage to give notice at work in order to focus on facing my fears.

During my final week of work I noticed that my thigh was numb. Were the symptoms an attempt to keep me locked into the status quo, like a child who is acting out? I chose to keep moving forward, numb thigh and all. I don't want to give you the impression that I was stoic about this...*I was terrified.*

People now see me as courageous. The complete opposite was true then, but I was committed to changing the family pathology for two reasons: Firstly, I felt that my body was screaming at me to get my attention, so maybe the symptoms would lessen and secondly, I felt that I had a Sacred obligation to change the pattern so *that my children would not have to carry it into the next generation.*

CHAPTER TWO
BRIDGE ACROSS FOREVER

"The hero must face the beginnings of change..."
Joseph Campbell

MY ANIMAL CLAN

Blog Entry : May 3. 2012

"Death and loss, they tear a hole in our hearts, but it is through this gaping hole that the winds of grace can pass."
— *Eckhart Tolle*

I don't know what it is with me and my animals, but something very strange goes on. After David and I began living together, we found we both had a love of horses. We visited horse farms on the weekend. I called them 'field trips'. I introduced David to an old friend who I'd met when raising my daughter. Her daughter and my daughter were friends.

Barbara had a beautiful horse farm. We reconnected in a deep way and began to ride her horses. She found David his first horse and she also connected me with Ransom. Ransom was a very tall handsome gelding who had an owner who was allegedly diagnosed with multiple personality disorder.

She had taken tremendous risks with him and they had fallen together going over jumps. He was known to be a bit skittish, however with me he was gentle and reliable. This perfectly demonstrates the ability horses have to mirror human behavior.

Once we attended an informal horse show, I sat on a tree stump while resting between classes and Ransom nuzzled my hair and put his lips on my shoulder. The other women laughed saying, *"he's in love with you!"*. I clearly felt his love and gratitude.

The expenses for this hobby were swiftly becoming too great to rationalize and we decided to purchase a small horse farm. We were more than casual enthusiasts and ready to take the next step. This was in 2001.

One day, Ransom shied and ran across the field. I went to run after him, but my legs would not go. I remember telling myself that I didn't need to run...*Denial.*

At the same time, something else was happening, when we rode Ransom he would kick out with his right leg. We called a veterinarian to look at him and Dr. Keith was very concerned. He wanted me to take Ransom to Baton Rouge to the LSU vet school. I loaded him in the horse trailer and drove him two hours to LSU.

Around this time, I'd developed optic neuritis, an inflammation of the optic nerve which is common in MS. When the LSU veterinarian saw Ransom, he suggested his wife take a look at him as well. She was an equine ophthalmologist and he felt there was something going on with Ransom's eyes.

I was not talking about my optic neuritis during this time and it was ironic when the equine ophthalmologist looked at Ranson's right optic nerve and called me over to look at it with her instrument, *"Look at that optic nerve, it is frayed!"*, she said. I was struggling to look at Ransom's optic nerve while my own optic nerve of the same eye was not focusing!

Suffice it to say that I had no idea what was happening with me or with him. As I became weaker, he became weaker - I eventually found him a home as a pet since he was no longer safe to ride.

I have to say that some of these entries are really painful to write...*the constant heartbreaks.* I feel like I've lived ten lifetimes. What is also true is once I've written this Story down it is out and I can let it go. Thanks to the blog gods for this catharsis, and I thank all of you for being willing and gracious witnesses!

Then something new happened, my stepson's girlfriend got a Great Dane puppy! I was very excited and heard that there was one left in the litter. When I called, the puppy was not available, but I had gotten the fever really bad and began looking on the Internet for a Great Dane puppy.

I found Basha in Victoria, British Columbia. An eight-week-old puppy who had never been away from her mother now flew from Victoria to Toronto to New Orleans. When I opened the crate a twenty-three-pound lion cub crawled out. She took one look around and crawled right back into her crate!

I hired a well-known dog trainer to help me train Basha as a service dog. Our horse farm was very busy with boarded horses, the horse's owners, clients from my psychology practice, our existing two dogs, chickens, ducks, roosters and a turkey. So Basha learned manners around other dogs, horses, and people. As she grew, and believe me she grew! She was socialized well and was my constant companion.

I would often say that Basha was not a dog. She was from a different species above humans. She came with me to women's groups and would, for example, comfort a grieving member. It took us a while to catch on, but once we realized she was *'working the group'* we found it hilarious.

Years later, when I had a nonviolent communication group. If someone was angry Basha would try to calm them by getting them to pet her and if that didn't work she would lie down in front of me. Between that person who was angry and me...*She always knew where I was.* She took her job very seriously.

On one devastating day on the horse farm. Our two other dogs, Isabel and Maggie, drank some antifreeze. At first I didn't know what it was, but I noticed that Isabel was walking funny. I called her over but she ran away. I had never seen the effects of antifreeze or I would've grabbed her immediately.

A few hours later I couldn't find Isabel and I went out in my golf cart to look around. Basha always came with me in my golf cart. Often I would look out of the window of my house and see the back of her head as she was sitting in the golf cart, waiting for a ride. Today however, we were on a serious mission together looking for Isabel!

We drove around the tree line and around the periphery of the property to the barns and shed, but couldn't find her. I was getting desperate and I said to Basha, *"Where is Isabel?"* And I'll be damned if she didn't jump out of the cart and dive into the tree line to show us where Isabel was... *where she was failing.*

David grabbed Isabel, I got her water and we rushed both dogs to an emergency veterinarian. After trying to revive Isabel and Maggie all night we had to euthanize them both. David held onto Maggie and I Isabel as the life went out of their eyes. We brought their bodies back to the farm and buried them in our animal graveyard.

A few days later, when I was alone in the house, I let out a wail. From the other side of the house I heard an echo, it was Basha with a reverberating Great Dane wail... *This was not a normal dog.*

On another day I was carrying my computer and I tripped. While reaching down in the attempt to save my computer, I fell to my knee and cracked my patella in half. Elsewhere, on the same day Basha was running with Dr. Keith's dog and tore her ACL in the same knee. I was on crutches and she was walking on three legs! Could this be a coincidence?

I had never experienced another being as committed to my well-being as this dog. As I became weaker, she supported me as I walked. I had a harness and held her on my right side, which was my weaker.

I went to renew my passport at the courthouse once, and there was a very long outdoor staircase. I'll never forget the rhythm we found walking up and down all those stairs. I held the railing with her on my other side. I took a step as she watched me, then she took a step. I took another step as she watched me, then she took a step. Her focus was 100% on me and the task at hand. The level of support this Being afforded me was immeasurable.

Once I fell down with my walker and couldn't get up. David was going to be away for another two hours, so I tried to get comfortable on the floor. Basha pushed her head against me to try to get me to get up. How would an animal know to do this?

When David moved out in 2008, Basha was beside herself, she was clearly grieving. At that time I was getting bee venom injections, and as I was getting my last injection, which was near my wrist. I made the statement, *"This one is really going to hurt"*. The exact moment the injection was given, Basha screamed from the next room and ran to us shaking. She shook for twenty minutes. I put her on herbal stress tabs and it took her a couple of months to work through her grief. Whether she was experiencing her own grief or my grief, I don't know, but she definitely tapped into...*The Grief.*

There were other instances that I could mention, but basically you got my drift. This was no dog.

THE LIE UNDERNEATH THE ILLNESS

Blog Entry : May 4. 2012

When someone has a significant illness, it can be that the physical body is trying to come into balance. I believe that this can be true of depression, addictions and anxiety as well. The greater the disruption, the greater the need for balance and wholeness. This is a shamanic perspective.

Shamanism is a method of healing where the practitioner accesses the spirit world to mend the soul, which can then help the body to heal. When my symptoms began, I embarked on a path to deeper levels of *'spiritual intimacy'* by closely observing my thoughts, my dream state, my meditation state and I slowly became aware of recurring themes.

There is an expression that I heard in my mind while awaking one morning that became prophetic, *"With the symptoms comes the Renaissance."*

Around that time, I had a vision. I saw two little hands on either side of my face, and a child's face looking into mine from a three-inch distance. She wanted me to look at her with no distractions. I knew this was a message from my *'inner child'*. Soon after, I began having many dreams of infants and toddlers. These children were dirty and unkempt.

In one dream I was at a swimming pool and I'd forgotten where the child was. I was terrified that because of my negligence she could have drowned. These dreams continued for a few years.

As I began to heal the fragments inside, the child dreams shifted. Later dreams presented a child who was clean and felt more connected to me. After a few more years, there was love and bonding between the child and me. It is interesting that my biological children had the same complaint about me, that I was distracted and they wanted more time with me.

Often times the clues to our healing are all around us if we are willing to see them and to see them we have to be willing to change. If we don't hear the clues initially, they will be repeated until we do. The nudge will be light at first, but will soon become more demanding. I seem to have needed a sledgehammer to get my attention many times.

I have found that my healing happens in layers and I have recently gotten to another layer. What has been wanting my attention lately has had to do with an issue related to my *Caregivers.*

Sometimes there is a pattern that we think we understand and once we work deeply with it the opposite is really true. I have such a pattern...*and it started in utero.*

My mother was a very strong woman. When she developed cancer my whole world was shaken. My internal story line was, *"she is my rock, how could I possibly be okay without her?"*. At the time I was doing deep energy work. One day a light bulb went off and I realized that the opposite was true. I had been *her* rock all of these years!

When this became clear, all my life relationships shifted and I saw that there was a similar truth about all of my significant relationships. I had thought that I was the weaker one in the relationship, while in reality I had been the one taking care of the other. My body had to break down for me to be able to see this.

The more I delved into this truth, the more I saw that this was the lie on which the whole illness was built. In meditations, I've seen repeatedly the ways that this *'turnaround'*, as Byron Katie calls it, was being presented to me but I had been either unwilling or unable to see it in the past.

I can remember over twenty years ago when a psychiatrist turned guru presented me with this truth and I saw it for a moment. My whole body started shaking and I couldn't speak for about twenty minutes. The truth wanted out, but I was not ready.

In recent months, as I have become more vulnerable physically, I've hired caregivers. Again, I began to take care of my caregivers. The pattern was insidious. I started to have the 'child dreams' again.

This time, in a dream, I was home and taking care of business when somebody brought a child over to my house. I suddenly realized that I did not know where the child had gone. I ran all over, desperately looking, feeling like I was in trouble. I then realized that I was not responsible for this child. The message was to stop taking care of other people's lost children. Okay, I get it!

So when I find myself becoming over involved in this way, I repeat the mantra, *"I am not responsible for your child"*.

Whenever I do this I let go a bit more and it is a huge relief *every time.*

FOUR ELEMENTS

Finding an anchored place within
Allows for the necessary wandering
Beyond the confines of the existing way
To test the water and confront the rigidity
Extinguishing the illusion
Only to find more illusion

The spiraling quest
For a deeper expression
Like the incoming breath
That lines the hall
And expires to the moon and her silhouette

All that was is changed
With the quake of the earth
And torched with a compassionate hand
Returns to the place
Where dragonfly rests
And communes with brother moon

THE GENESIS

Blog Entry : May 8. 2012

I was in my late twenties when I first joined Yokefellow - a therapeutic community based in New Orleans, and I was in a tumultuous and violent marriage. I didn't realize at first how unconventional the therapists at Yokefellow were nor how they would initiate my inner work - a process that would continue for most of my adult life.

Patricia and Ken, who ran Yokefellow, co-facilitated intensive group psychotherapy that had transactional analysis at its foundation and utilized Arthur Janov's Primal Scream. Gestalt therapy and a variation of what they called 're-parenting'. It was not unusual to see baby bottles in the therapy room nor clients planning to enact their desired and evolved 'chosen' birth processes. The Yokefellow community was composed of nearly fifty people, and as was common with all of my teachers, they were controversial in the mainstream community!

During my initial appointments with these co-facilitators, they appeared caring, seasoned and 'present'. Ken was wearing khaki pants and a long-sleeved shirt rolled up at the wrists. Nothing appeared to be out of the ordinary. But as I began intensive group therapy, I began to notice a few irregularities.

Physical contact is something that is gravely lacking in our society. Personally, my father had been very demonstrative and my mother very distant. In this new setting, I noticed an unusual practice in that people arranged ahead of time who was going to sit next to Patricia, *"I get her left side," "I get her right side," "I get the wishbone!"*

My first reaction was that this practice was ridiculous. I felt I was 'above the fray'. The thought of choosing to sit close to Patricia was not even on my radar and vying for a position was probably my greatest nightmare! This is all a perfect demonstration of *how the Shadow manifests*.

After a few sessions of group psychotherapy I began to notice something unusual about the other facilitator, Ken. Ken sometimes wore T-shirts which revealed multiple tattoos all over his body, and this was way before tattoos were mainstream.

I began to hear more about his colorful biography. He was quite forthcoming about his history and given his professionalism and effectiveness as a therapist. I was intrigued by his Story.

THE STORY OF KEN

Ken had grown up in California, and his father was a convict. Ken had been involved with drugs and many run-ins with the law. During the Vietnam war, he found himself in Marion prison, a maximum security prison in Marion, Illinois.

At the same time, Marty Groder, a Jewish psychiatrist, was placed in Marion prison for a year to avoid going to Vietnam. When Dr. Groder arrived he found that the system was flawed. As the story goes, the warden was crazy, the inmates were crazy, the trustees were crazy, and the only way he was going to stay sane for the next year was to make other people sane.

Dr. Groder began conducting confrontation oriented group therapy sessions with the inmates in which Ken was a member. He began confronting Ken about being a punk - with his dark shades, tattoos and felonious behavior. It is also notable that Ken was not a typical inmate. Ken was well read in esoteric subjects and was practicing a form of meditation that he believed would make the walls and the bars disappear if he concentrated hard enough!

Ken became intrigued with Marty Groder's persistent and penetrating approach, and the intrigue morphed into respect. Ken became enrolled in the mission to 'make people sane', and he began an apprenticeship under Marty's tutelage. essentially earning a psychiatric degree without the doctoral program.

They called the approach the Askelepian Game, a name derived from the ancient Greek mystery schools in Askelepious. In Ken's words, as he took down the walls within himself, the walls outside of him literally disappeared. He was up for parole before his apprenticeship was completed. In his words, the system wanted to spit him out as fast as it could. He had become way too healthy for the insanity of the prison system!

Having a therapist with a resume like that, how could I not flourish? I don't want to minimize what it took for me to keep showing up for the demands of this rigorous path. It demanded everything from me, and this continues to the present.

Considering the complex choices I was going to have to make in my life, this experience gave me the foundation for negotiating the challenges of parenting, co-parenting, step parenting, and on. In spite of the deprivation of my early years, I was committed to give and receive more love in my life and to provide more for my children than my parents were ever capable of...*hoping my children could progress beyond me.*

As I was finding my own way, I also needed to be an example to others in my personal and professional community. Sometimes I was the teacher, sometimes my children taught me and many times my clients taught me. As Hillary Clinton once said, *"it takes a village."* Isn't that the *truth?*

UNCLE

Blog Entry : May 10, 2012

I was a willful and stubborn child, and one of the qualities people seem to like most about me is my steadfastness. I have a tendency to be very determined in my beliefs. When I seize on a protocol or a treatment plan I won't give up until I have completed it or I believe it is ineffective... *sometimes both are true.*

After twenty years of proactivity regarding this illness, I am beginning to wonder whether the trajectory can even be altered. Perhaps the teaching involves the means employed and my attitude towards those means, rather than the end result.

When I say, *"people seem to like that about me",* that isn't completely true. I do remember power struggles with other willful people, and I remember the frustration people have experienced who really care about me. I can cry at that and of course, these patterns will always be more apparent with parents, children *and spouses.*

When I think about it logically, it makes perfect sense to plan a curriculum to treat dogged (sorry Basha) determination by setting up circumstances that cannot be altered by will. Imagine the benefit of becoming okay with chaos, or being out of control, *perhaps it is in the surrendering of will where true power is manifested.*

This can be a slippery slope because I can seize the opportunity to try to control a situation in a counterintuitive way, but maturing on a spiritual level demands integrity. As Maya Angelou says, *"when you know better, you do better"*. To know better and to not do better would be a breach of integrity. I think I'm beginning to know better.

If my theory is correct, and I have created a curriculum as challenging as this appears, I must be kick-ass courageous! I believe in my heart of hearts that the Universe is a safe and loving place. That can be my only interpretation.

ASIDE

With this illness many doctors' appointments have ended in dead ends, and much to my unending frustration. After months of recurring uterine tract infections, two hospitalizations, a fractured ankle and much suffering, I was ready to say...*Uncle!*

February, 1995

LIBERATION

Blog Entry : May 14, 2012

Once when younger, I was in an abusive relationship. He drank a lot of alcohol and called me disrespectful and hurtful names. He knocked me down a few times and when I tried to stand up to him the results were even more severe. I was totally clueless about how to deal with this situation. I'd become an abused wife. I didn't stay in the situation for very long *but more than five minutes was way too much!*

As my mind cleared, I said to myself, *"now that I am out of it I can help others".* I learned how I did not want to live. I thought it was over and a part of my past. I understand that this experience could never have happened if there wasn't something in me that mirrored that behavior, kind of like a receptor, I say this with no self blame...*none,* but I've also learned that that 'something' inside of me *has continued the pattern.*

With the illness, I've had to look closely at my 'internal conversations', *"How did I create this?" "What legacy am I leaving my children?" "Did my fears attract this illness?"* Thirty years later, I see the same perpetrator in different clothing, but the voice is more cunning. *"Have I manifested this?"* almost sounds spiritual...*but true spiritual messages are not harsh.*

Something that needs to be released has remained intact. I hear the self-centeredness in all of these statements. Even seemingly true spiritual teachings can brutalize - *the perpetrator is within.* Had that not been the case, there would've been no opening for abusive behavior in relationships to take root. I've often wondered why I couldn't just walk away from the situation as I have seen others do. There was an opening that I needed to become aware of but had I not experienced that situation, I would have never seen the present reenactment. You cannot change what you don't acknowledge.

It takes so much courage to live with your eyes open. People willing to read these writings are of this category... *We are in good company.*

MY FATHER'S GREATEST TEACHING

Blog Entry : May 22, 2012

My daughter Casey was a toddler when my father was diagnosed with prostate cancer. I remember that because the recommended treatment at the time was implanting a radium seed in the prostate and I had to be vigilant to keep Casey away from him for a while to avoid radiation exposure. Vigilance was not difficult for me when it came to my children's well-being.

At that point my father was in his late sixties. During his mid-eighties, he decided that he no longer needed the medication. I don't remember whether this decision was questioned, but soon after medical testing revealed a recurrence of the cancer.

If you knew my father, you might know that he was a staunch atheist, though I didn't know that fact for most of my life. During his eighties my father began talking about his early years as a socialist. Apparently he went to a socialist school. I didn't realize there were schools for communists and socialists!

As my father became more ill I was visiting him every few months from Louisiana. The next to last time I visited, while I was walking him to the dinner table. My mother told me this was a very rare occurrence in those days. My father must have been reflecting on what was on all our minds. He said, *"they are just going to put me in the ground and that is it...and anybody who thinks otherwise is sentimental."* I remember this statement like it was yesterday. This was the philosophy I grew up with.

During his decline, I was in intensive breathwork training in Sedona, Arizona for four weeks. I remember getting daily reports from my mother and talking to the breathwork trainer who had recently lost her father. She recommended a classic book in dealing with end-of-life issues titled *Final Gifts*, which was written by two hospice workers.

When I returned home to Louisiana, I had a significant dream. It was elaborate and I recorded it at the time. I was riding in a vehicle which was going way too fast down an exit ramp in a parking garage. There was a monkey driving who was obviously out of his mind.

What I had been confronting in myself was this tendency to overanalyze and get lost in my mental chatter. This dream was a message that I needed to discipline the 'monkey mind'. a Buddhist term for unbridled, undisciplined thought that wreaks havoc and competes with *'living in the heart'*, and I was on a mission to live more in my heart and intuition than in my mind.

I remember that that happened on a Friday and my brother, Dale, was arriving on Saturday to visit. I had a strong intuition to visit my father, I called my mother and told her how I felt. She told me that my father was extremely medicated and wasn't at all aware of his environment. I urged that I still felt the need to visit him, and in exasperation she said to me, *"okay I will put him on the phone"* When he heard my voice he said to me, *"Hello doll, are you coming over?"..."Yes dad, I'm coming now,"* I replied, and I drove directly to the airport.

I brought with me on the airplane the book I mentioned, *Final Gifts*, to read. A woman at the opposite end of my row enthusiastically acknowledged it, saying, *"I am a hospice worker and my daughter's friends wrote that book!."* Okay, I felt like I was in the zone!

That evening I arrived at my brother and sister-in-law's house in Pennsylvania to sleep for the night. In the morning I visited my father, and when he saw me he asked me how long I was going to stay. I told him that I'd be there for about a day. He responded by saying, *"Oh good, you will be available in case I need you".* This was the man who was supposedly not in touch with reality.

Within a few hours he began his dying process. We called hospice and I called Dale to come home. With the help of the promptings from the book I was reading, I sat with my father as he shared his experience as best he could from the intermittent times he was spending on 'the other side'. I asked him if his mother visited and he happily shared, *"she comes to see me every day, she loves to come see me."*

What shocked me the most was when he talked about *Heaven*. When I expressed shock to hear him speak of heaven, thinking that I did not understand the word he explained, *"it is a place of tranquility".* If I ever had doubts about the spirit world, I no longer do. Thank you father for your greatest teaching!

After that exchange, my brothers, sisters-in-law and I stood around my father's bed for hours. Unable to bear the scene, my mother came in separately to say her goodbyes. It was unnerving when my father began to struggle and choke, but the hospice nurse reassured us that it was part of the process.

I stroked my father's forehead and sang *"Child of God"*... a song I'd sung to my son Jordan every night for his first ten years of life. I was becoming anxious as the night wore on and my father continued to struggle. I asked my brother Lee to sleep nearer to my father's room in case things worsened. So Lee slept on one side of the house and I slept in my parents room on the other. At 3:00 a.m., within five minutes of each other, we walked into my father's room where he lay peacefully. He took one more breath as I held his hand. I looked above his body and said goodbye to the man who gave me life.

ACROSS THE BRIDGE OF HOPE

Blog Entry : May 17, 2012

"A friend is someone who knows the song in your heart, and will sing it back to you when you have forgotten the words."
- Donna Roberts

In 2001, my close friends Diana and Mark gathered with a few friends at Loyola University in New Orleans to sing gospel music together and after a few weeks I joined them.

My voice was adequate, not well-trained, but had a lot of heart. I had taken voice lessons from an accomplished soprano a decade earlier and was directed to the soprano section which included two or three other women on a good night.

One Thursday night, my worst fear was realized. I was the only soprano present. I was the soprano section! My friends knew how horrified I was of this and Mark, who sang tenor with the New Orleans Opera, stood up with me and sang the soprano part with me! This generosity was classically Mark. He has been my best male friend in life. As the disease progressed, choir members strategically stood around me in case I lost my balance.

Thetius stood on my left side and had a booming soprano voice that was obviously trained since childhood in an African-American church choir. Initially, as I was trying to loosen my throat and register a few notes. I looked toward

Thetius for guidance. I asked her to direct my pitch if I were sharp or flat and she would point her finger up or down. I thanked her profusely. She said to me, *"Girl, we all gots to help each other!"* When she said that I cried, and I knew that I was in the right place!

With no further ado, our first singing engagement was scheduled...*September 12, 2001!* After the bombing of the World Trade Center on the previous day, we wondered whether the date should be postponed.

It became clear to us that having our performance the day after this tragedy was no accident. As we sang in the small chapel in Trinity Church, the overwhelming response clarified our mission of 'solidarity among differences' and for the next five years I participated in the '**Shades of Praise New Orleans Interracial Gospel Choir**'.

Our choir performed at churches, synagogues, The New Orleans Jazz Festival, political events, and the St. Louis Cathedral just to name a few venues! Some of our voices were individually breathtaking, but our collective voice was deeply moving for many people. We even recorded a number of CDs. Wherever our unifying and joyful message was needed, we were there!

In 2003, one of the organizers from the choir got an invitation for us to go on tour in Ireland. It was an opportunity to spread our message of solidarity in a country divided by sectarianism. We flew to Dublin the exact night that US troops were entering Afghanistan. I remember watching the military maneuvers on television in the Dublin airport. Many of us were horrified, this was the polar opposite of our mission...*to bring people together in harmony.*

From Dublin we rode on a tour bus to Omagh, a city in Northern Ireland where a car bombing had taken place and killed many men women and children on August 15, 1998. The hatred inherent in sectarianism had emotionally devastated this town.

We stayed in private homes in the community and heard the heartbreaking stories first-hand. Netflix has 'Omagh: The Legacy'. It is good, but a documentary cannot quite capture what we experienced personally when bonding intimately with these people.

Our entire experience in Ireland was life-changing, but our time in Omagh the most profoundly so. We toured the town and spoke about racism and sectarianism. We broke bread with the families, performed in both of their churches respectively - as catholics and protestants did not intermingle - and witnessed the broken pavement where the car bomb exploded. But the best part was our joint concert.

In Omagh, after the car bombing, a high school choir had come together made up of catholic and protestant adolescents. This was very unusual as the students were educated separately and essentially lived parallel lives. The Duchess of Abercorn sponsored the choir and their courageous mission of peace and reconciliation. In preparation for our visit, 'Shades of Praise' learned their theme song 'Bridge Across Forever' and we surprised them by singing it for them in our concert! We also sang with them...*and our missions were joined.*

Once, as we swiftly jogged to the high school for our practice with the choir, I began to show a visible limp for the first time. I remember walking with Mark on one side of me and Diana on the other. The support from my friends and my choir was exactly what I needed at that moment. We continued to perform throughout Northern Ireland and the Republic of Ireland.

We went to the home of the president of Northern Ireland, the Duke and Duchess of Abercorn, as well as many other historic places. We ended the week with a powerful performance at an old church in Dublin.

Everyone in the church, young and old, well and disabled, stood and held hands. It was a moving way to end the most profound adventure of my life.

I returned from Ireland to complete medical testing, which resulted in a multiple sclerosis diagnosis. 2003 was a tumultuous yet profound year that would change my life forever.

PASS THE PRUNE JUICE, DAMMIT

Blog Entry : May 24, 2012

I think I'm beginning to understand the psychology of grumpy people. You put a person in a situation of 'learned helplessness', then render them even more helpless and you've got the ingredients for a very unhappy individual - and one who makes other people equally unhappy.

This morning I blasted a benevolent individual who was just trying to do her job. Because the urinary tract infection has recurred, I am in another 'skilled nursing facility' for a ten day stay. I did not want to subject myself to yet another traumatic experience of this kind, but under pressure from my family, I yielded.

It had taken me a whole year to extend my sleep time to over three hours - seven hours of sleep is the minimum recommended amount - and it was the third time somebody had awakened me in the middle of the night in this facility. I don't feel good about my outburst, but sometimes *"life just works on your last nerve"*...as they say in New Orleans.

By nature, I'm a pleasant and self-sufficient person. Contrary to what my husbands believe, I'm not an individual overly involved with feelings of 'entitlement'. I am sure that my development in the face of unimaginable adversity has contributed to this even-temperedness over time. Twenty years in the trenches researching, implementing, and researching again without remission of symptoms has led me to become a boiling cauldron of frustration when certain stressors are presented.

Twenty years of dealing with an illness that appears to be intransigent no matter what measures are taken, including completely changing diet, sleep patterns, supplementation, medications, stem cell treatment, and that barely scratches the surface, can lead to either complete exasperation or unfathomable blind faith. For me, deep psychological and spiritual practices have helped to tip the balance in the direction of the latter.

This is in contrast with a lifelong pattern of deferring my power to others, which has led to confusion regarding the direction I've needed to take for my own evolution. As long as I can remember, I have been deferring my power to an authority outside of myself. And each significant recurrence of that pattern has seemed to result in a dramatic progression of the illness. This tendency seems paradoxical given the suggestion that I was too willful.

How do I juggle these opposites, bring awareness and develop a plan to grow through this seeming paradox? How do I process through this...*consciously and kindly*, yet also with the fierce determination necessary to finally eradicate this conundrum?

Finding this balance between willfulness and autonomy seems to be my work. And, what seems most important is that when there is a transgression, like outrage stemming from sleep deprivation at 5 a.m, it is essential that one *acknowledges* the error and corrects the behavior, with the essential ingredient of self-forgiveness *or self-empathy* figuring prominently in the mix.

The way I've done that internally is to acknowledge the feeling that was triggered and then feel the grief associated with the wound, make amends for my outburst and forgive myself.

Not knowing oneself and therefore not being able to meet one's own needs is a set up for disgruntled behavior. Empathy as opposed to judgment is called for in these circumstances.

I understand that this process is a part of the legacy my mother left me, one she didn't have the opportunity to learn of for herself. My mother was known to be a grumpy person. So I guess dealing with this legacy...*was not part of her curriculum this time around.*

Returning to a nursing facility has been a major stressor for me. I need to take that into account and give myself a break *and not in the form of an ankle fracture this time!*

MAMA MIA

Blog Entry : May 25, 2012

My relationship with my mother was complicated.

She was first generation American-born and her father had emigrated from Lithuania when he was in the single digits. After his sister made enough money to bring him over by working in a sweatshop in lower Manhattan, he grew up to marry another immigrant. My mother was the only daughter of four children.

When she met my father, he was lighthearted and physically demonstrative. My mother was drawn to this quality like a moth to the light.

Most of my mother's family had been killed in *"the war"*. I remember a photograph of a large family with many children, most of them deceased. As a small child I looked into the faces of these children and wondered how this could possibly be true.

I don't think my mother was prepared for having a family. She probably would have been a successful businesswoman if she had been educated. She had been advanced a few grades in elementary school because of her innate intelligence and she went to college for a short period, but women had very few options at that time.

So at nineteen years old she had a husband and a baby. When I think about it now, I imagine she was in the proverbial meat grinder emotionally. I suspect that by the time I arrived she was burned out. Within nine years she had three children and was over her head.

My mother was more suited to be a blackjack dealer then to be a mother and wife. Her father allegedly ran numbers in the Bronx. I'm not sure what that means, but he knew all the Yankee players on a first name basis and placed bets and had a lot of pieces of paper. He always had a cigar in his mouth and a transistor radio up to his ear.

For most of my childhood my mother was ill with something mysterious. It made her less available and more self-centered as she had to navigate serious health issues. My family experienced much deprivation. Perhaps that accounts for the many addictions that manifested later.

In 2006, when my mother was gravely ill, my siblings thought it necessary for me to fly to Pennsylvania to say goodbye. She had pneumonia and was not expected to survive the week. I flew by myself from Louisiana to Pennsylvania in a wheelchair. They didn't tell my mother that I was coming in case I couldn't manage the flight.

When I wheeled into my mother's room I saw a look on her face that I had never seen before, especially directed at me. It was a profound look of love and excitement. Until that moment I had never really believed that my mother loved me...*never*. To this day this wonderful look is how she appears to me in my meditations. My mother recovered from that bout of pneumonia to survive a few more years.

During 2010, Casey's future in-laws came to my home in Colorado for the weekend to meet me. We had a lovely weekend together and on our last night I got that fateful telephone call... *mother had passed.*

The following morning, my children prepared to begin their journey to Pennsylvania where the funeral would take place. Due to the level of difficulty for me to travel, I chose to say my goodbyes in a more solitary and personal way.

The arms are falling
The arms that lost the baby
The baby is crying
For the loss of the mother

A circle of grief
Surrounds the family
No one can talk about it
No one can tell
Where the deepest hole comes from

And in the dark recesses
A flame was extinguished
Without oxygen and food

No one can survive

There's a glimmer of hope
On a southwestern mountain
A beating heart
And a warm summer glow

Reminds me
Of my love for the people
And an unfinished journey
To rekindle the flame

Do I dare hope for fulfillment
Where disappointment may be part of the plan
Can I possibly open some fingers
And free-fall downward

Not knowing what's there?

ASIDE

Nina, my primary caregiver at the time, assisted me into bed. I happened to look at a white surface next to my bed and I saw a black dot.

To my horror I shrieked, *"Is that a tick?"*. Nina quickly replied, *"No.. well..."*...And she took it between her nails and squeezed it and said, *"well it's dead now."*

So, In the middle of the Colorado winter, at the end of December, there was a deer tick next to my bed. To give this context, the form of multiple sclerosis that I have been struggling with for almost twenty years which can stem from multiple opportunistic infections or Lyme disease...*which is carried by a deer tick!*

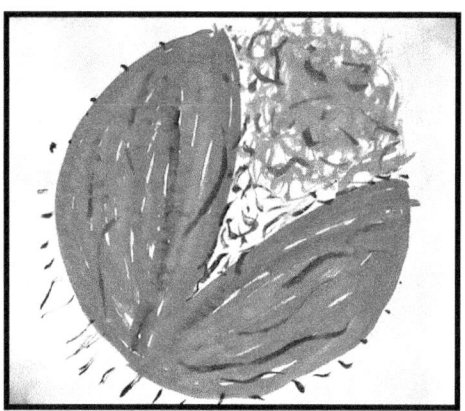

Taos - February, 2001

CHAPTER THREE

THE GREAT PURIFIER

"The hero commits to the adventure..." Joseph Campbell

INTEGRATION OF THE FEMININE: THE KEYSTONE

Blog Entry : June 6, 2012

* keystone – a central, cohesive source of support and stability; the central supporting element of a whole.

I've had two significant revelations recently.

The first was that the urinary tract infection has recurred. I suspected that it would come back because my bladder is not emptying completely and there's an area that holds stagnation. When I asked the doctor if she thought the outcome would be different this time she responded, *"I don't know"*. She increased the dosage of the antibiotic and my family felt strongly that I should comply, so I did.

I hoped that it would work, but it didn't. I was quite devastated in spite of expecting that negative outcome. I see the urologist tomorrow and that will be my last medical appointment in Pennsylvania. I hope he will have some suggestions for dealing with the stagnation.

The second revelation involved *'the old woman archetype'* that I've been working with for the last decade. It became clear that I've been trying to *'complete this energy'*, or in some way bring it to an end - that the 'archetype' was a negative directive and needed to be exorcised.

During my meditations last night *She*, in the workings of my mind's eye, was invited to join my circle of guides and family. My guides pointed out the error of my strategy and it felt like *Truth*. As soon as I initiated this shift - this 'inviting' of the archetype, instead of rejecting it - an entire layer of grief was released. When I think of how long I have been pushing this energy away I am humbled at how blind I could be.

When the tick appeared, which I described in the blog entry Mama Mia, the desire to push this energy away escalated. However, when I accepted the energy of the old woman archetype...*the relief I experienced was profound.* I realized that this 'reframing' and the subsequent integration of this mysterious crone energy was the *keystone* to the structure of my healing work.

Now, as I spend time in meditation, I begin to honor the positive attributes of the old woman. What I've realized is that she represents aspects of myself that I had to *grow into* in order to wake up each day and live my life in this particular costume with this particular role. I needed to integrate her courage. She represents the wisdom earned from a very demanding curriculum that sometimes makes me want to scream. If this were not the case, they wouldn't call it courage. She also represents the wounding of the Feminine for many generations in my family.

A BRAZILIAN MYSTERY

Blog Entry : June 12, 2012

Today I discussed exit strategies with my daughter. It is not a conversation many people get to share, but my daughter and I are not ordinary people.

JOHN OF GOD

Casey and I went together to see a healer named 'John of God', who works his healing in the village of Abadiania in Brazil. During this trip, I saw clearly, really for the first time, the nature of my relationship with my daughter. This village was a place unlike any I have visited.

At the far end of the trip, while leaving, John of God's demeanor led me to determined that healing this illness was not likely...*that perhaps there was another plan.* While Casey had an impressive healing, mine was more in the psychological and spiritual realms. Welcome to my world of healing!

In his village, Abadiania, we walked like pilgrims en masse, clothed in white to see John of God. We stood in line and he gave his interpreter instructions for each visitor. Casey and I were to go for 'psychic surgery' first thing in the morning.

The next morning we entered the room where the healing happens, and after a mysterious process were instructed to go back to our 'cassitas'. We slept for twenty hours straight.

The atmosphere in the village was ecstatic. We saw people let go of their wheelchairs, their walking canes and the like. In our little cassita, in such close quarters, Casey and I reworked our relationship for the first time *by ourselves*, without the help of therapists or friends.

For the first couple days she was angry and accusatory - all for good reasons. I was able to listen, take it in and *acknowledge* her perspective for the first time. By the fourth day Casey and I were laughing hysterically about anecdotal circumstances during her childhood!

Casey and I left our two-week adventure in Brazil with a clearer sense of who we were individually as well as in relationship with one another. Whether any physical healing happened for me in that unique Brazilian village or not, our relationship was much lighter and joyful!

THE ASKLEPIAN GAME

Blog Entry : June 16, 2012

Having been involved in an intimate community committed to integrity in thought, word and deed. I learned a lot about human nature in others and in myself. I learned how a lack of awareness and immaturity can become manifested in such a way that it *erodes intimacy.*

There were many times in the community when people had interpersonal conflict. These conflicts were dealt with honestly and honorably. After working through many such issues, I began to release a critical mass of shame that was triggered in the conflicts. I began to live a life with a much more profound level of transparency.

Instead of feeling defensive when there was conflict, I learned to believe that we were all human beings - with our lower ego selves. But when given a choice, we often choose the high road. Believing in this deeper sense of goodness in people has helped me with sticky personal relationships, both personally and professionally.

To me it is all about awareness. If people are willing to become more aware, paths of communication are much less problematic.

'THE GAME'

'The Asklepian Game', or *'The Game'* as we call it, is a highly confrontational model - one that provides a mirror in which to see one's blockages to authenticity.

The Game usually ran from Friday night to Sunday evening. There were plenty of openings for someone to become mean-spirited or the opposite, *manipulatively victimized*, but if this happened the person would usually be confronted with this behavior.

This process was very useful in learning about your defense mechanisms and how they blocked your authenticity. It destabilized one's personality structure. To make it through Saturday a healthy foundation to the personality was required.

Those of us who did The Game regularly recognized the challenge and wondered who would return Saturday morning after the opening night. If you made it until Saturday afternoon, you would usually make it through Sunday!

To give you an example of what was possible during this process I will offer my experience of reconciling with my estranged husband during one of these weekends.

I had been separated for over a year from my first husband, Eric. We were not seeing each other due to the level of conflict between us, yet we were unwilling to let go of the marriage. It was particularly hard for me to justify a complete severance because we had a child together.

Our relationship was deeply problematic and abusive. However, as with most complicated relationships, there was a lot to be learned and healed both separately and between us. I frequently felt victimized by him and would often give away my power. What I came to see was that I really didn't know which came first, my sense of powerlessness or his abuse. I began to see that I had complicity in the abuse. When I realized that I was part of the problem, I also realized that I was part of the solution!

At first I acted, in The Game, like a powerless mouse who was being victimized but I found my voice in this sacred space. Being surrounded by people who supported me in breaking this pattern was of great assistance.

The phrase 'ruthless support' was born at The Game. At one point I was standing on a chair speaking at the top of my lungs to Eric. I made him hear me. On his part, he was able to see what was in the way of his hearing me and a sense of respect for me was re-evoked - something that had been missing for quite some time.

After clearing away much of the pathological patterns in our relationship, the love we had originally connected with remained. We then did what people were later encouraged not to do, we made a life decision based on the expanded consciousness provided by The Game and reconciled our marriage.

From this process I clearly saw that, as long as we were clear with each other, there was enough love to support the relationship. Since then, I've taken this information to future relationships and it has helped me to not recreate the same pitfalls. I matured immensely from this process but my relationship with Eric devolved again after a few years.

By seeing the blocks in the way of opening my heart, and by walking through the process of leaving the blocks behind, I learned how to consciously open my heart more effectively than with any other process I've experienced.

It would be easy to demonize the teaching once I had come to the end of its usefulness in my life, but as with most things, to throw the baby out with the bath water would be to sacrifice something important in myself.

"When you know better you do better" (Maya Angelou). I feel very fortunate to have found so many helpers along the way to help me to *know better* and that has helped me to go on and help other people know better as well.

CO-MADRE HONOR: THE SACRED TRIANGLE

Blog Entry : June 21, 2012

Nearly two decades ago, I went to a "Horses and Healing" Conference in San Antonio, Texas.

At the conference I met a beautiful Latina woman who was instructed to saddle a Peruvian gelding with me. As we curried his body together we shared stories about our lives. She talked about her family members and referred to her 'co-madre' when describing a dear relative in her family. When I looked confused she went on to explain this sacred relationship.

She said that in her culture there was a special relationship between the two women who were grandparents to a particular child and that this sharing was considered a *sacred honor.*

I have had many auspicious **relationships with women.** When Sid and I connected, for example, he had a young teenage daughter who was a huge gift in my life.

Erica and her mother Linda had a good deal of conflict in their relationship and, as is the case with many teenage children, they need to live with the parent that has not been raising them consistently. Erica was no exception and I noticed that there was a deep fissure between Erica and her mother.

I saw how someone less aware could slip into their drama if she were living unconsciously. Instead, I felt the call to be a 'bridge' between them. Having been a family therapist for many years, I felt it was important to strengthen their bond.

In all fairness, I have to credit Erica for some of this. She affirmed my value in life and none of my own insecurities surfaced. And also in fairness, Linda was known to make this comment about me, *"If you don't like Ilene, there is something wrong with you"*. This was a good crew to practice conscious relationships with! Eventually, their bond strengthened and I can happily say there was never any animosity between us.

A few years later, Jerilyn came into my life. Jerilyn was a beautiful woman who later married Eric, Casey's father. I remember the first moment I met her. I was working as a sales manager at a furniture store in New Orleans and she and Eric walked in to pick up Casey. It was Valentine's Day and Eric had brought a heart-shaped box of chocolates for Casey.

The owner of the store walked in and said, *"who is that beautiful couple?"* I remember saying, *"That's not a beautiful couple, that is Casey's father!"* I was not as magnanimous as Linda had been in the beginning! When this beautiful woman told my daughter that she couldn't have chocolate until she had her lunch, I wanted to chime in, *"Yes Casey, go right ahead and eat as many chocolates as you would like!"* - to remind everybody who was the mother. Those are the kinds of things you say if your Shadow is in charge.

When I got to know Jerilyn, we became warm friends. When Sidney walked into the room and I was talking on the phone with Jerilyn, he would see me laughing hysterically and I would say that I was talking to my ex-wife-in law!

Through Casey's teenage years, Jerilyn provided a bridge for Casey and me. I remember feeling the similarity of dynamics as with Erica and Linda. History was repeating itself and I felt gratitude for this relationship between women with integrity and for this kind of help and helpfulness.

I knew that getting over one's 'smallness' to strengthen the child's primary relationship - that being 'unselfish' - was one of the most important functions of a step-parent. The Spanish term co-madre came up for me in my mind.

It was many years before I would enter into a relationship where I was a literal co-madre - as one of two biological grandmothers to Casey's child, River. Being as physically vulnerable as I am, however, makes me feel a bit vulnerable in this sacred triangle.

I feel the need for partnership, for tag-team participation. I cannot get on the floor and play with him, nor can I even hold or console him. I am reliant once again on another woman for help. And, also once again, I'm dealing with a woman who has sensitivity, courage and integrity. There is a beautiful dance that can happen when women are open and willing and I've had the privilege of being a part of a *Sacred Tag-Team of Co-Madres.*

HARALD AND BONNIE GOT IT GOING ON

Blog Entry : June 25, 2012

I listened to Bonnie Raitt this morning. Here are some of the lyrics:

"That was then and this is now, Found my way back here somehow, Take me down, You can hold me down, But you can't hold what's within me.

Someone other than who I am, I will fight to make my stand, Cause what is livin' if I can't live free, What is freedom if I can't be me.

Pull me around, Push me to the limit, Maybe I may bend, But I will not be broken."

Returning to Colorado was not the easiest thing to do, but it was the *right thing to do*. Here in the high desert, with extreme heat and with forest fires nearby, it is clearly the road less traveled! If you experience the town I live in you would understand the esoteric nature of my decision.

By definition Esoteric means, *'designed for or understood by the specially initiated alone.'*

Sometimes even I don't understand why I would choose to live alone in the wilderness. Although the town is isolated, I feel less isolated in Crestone than in Scranton or anywhere else right now.

This is the room where I do my physical therapy.

Certainly most of my family and friends don't understand. I suspect that there are clues in the song:

"I will fight to make my stand"

Living in the desert at 8000 feet altitude is not easy, especially if you have compromised breathing capabilities. Just breathing can be a struggle on certain days, and add to that smoke from the forest fires affecting the air quality.

"What is living if I can't live free what is is freedom if I can' t be me?"

That about says it.

On the other hand, my internet connection just became DSL and my Skype conversations have much clearer reception. More grocery stores have opened with competitive prices for organic produce and the most effective physical therapist I have ever met comes right to my house.

Harald, originally from Germany, was referred to me after my femur fracture. *"This is your lucky day,"* the person referring him said as she gave me his number.

It was 2007 and I was still in the hospital when I placed my call to him. I mentioned the femur, but neglected to mention the neurological issues. When he first met me, Harald was surprised to learn the complications of my case.

Dancing with Harald in 2008

But that didn't intimidate Harald, and for the next three years we worked together through my separation and divorce, through the ups and downs of this illness and our respective learning curves.

We laughed together and cried together, and we weathered the celebrations and heartbreaks.

Last month I e-mailed Harald for an appointment. I briefly described my double ankle fractures and we experienced déjà vu. We hadn't seen each other for two years and it had been a difficult two years for me. Harald devised the treatment plan in his mind and said, *"okay, let's stand,"* and with some thought he added, *"but first, let me hold your hand"* and our hearts got on board.

Yes, five years after I originally moved to Crestone, I am still fighting to make a stand, Bonnie, but this time *I am bringing my heart along.*

ADDENDUM TO LAST ENTRY

Blog Entry : June 27, 2012

I wanted to offer an addendum to my last blog entry, *Harald and Bonnie.*

In the lyrics of her song, Bonnie Raitt sings, *"I will fight to make a stand"* and I think it is important to note that war terminology is not really what I am comfortable with when speaking about the illness curriculum.

For many years, in spite of the semantics involved, I did wage a war of sorts and with every battle I had to retreat and regroup but if my theory is correct, and I am learning to let go of willfulness and embrace *Faith*, the teaching has been fruitful.

Marianne Williamson wrote a beautiful quote regarding this in her book *Returning to Love*: *"Attacking a disease is not a cure. Attacking a disease only makes it yell louder. Healing comes from entering into a conversation with our illnesses, seeking to understand what it's trying to tell us."*

I like to bring this philosophy to all of the energies that seem to be in conflict with *'The Source'*, whether they be illnesses, addictions or even a difference of opinion. Marshall Rosenberg, PhD, the recipient of the *Bridge of Peace Award*, has a wonderful body of work which helps bring harmony and mutuality to differences. His work is a good resource for the study of 'nonviolent communication.'

KATRINA: THE GREAT PURIFIER

Blog Entry : June 30, 2012

On August 23, 2005, after twenty-five years of hurricane preparation and hearing that someday...*"if a hurricane hit New Orleans 'just so' the water from Lake Pontchartrain would overtake the levees",* Hurricane Katrina flooded the city of New Orleans.

We were living on our horse farm about fifty minutes north of New Orleans. Our farm was a refuge for friends evacuating the city and lakefront area during hurricane season. On August 22, our dearest friends Mark and Diana - who lived within ten blocks of Lake Pontchartrain - arrived with cases of spring water, wine, assorted batteries, a windup radio and food from the freezer that needed to be eaten before it went bad. They also brought local family members including a sister, brother-in-law and their eighty-five year old mother.

We lost power during the hurricane, so we took turns winding the radio - if you wound it sixty times you earned two minutes of radio time. At first we had no clue about the level of devastation and suffering that was happening a mere fifty miles away.

One of our friends drove her horse to us from a more vulnerable stable in New Orleans before the contraflow of traffic reversed, and she was barely able to get back in time to evacuate her family.

We only had a day or two to secure a generator to run the water pump or the horses would have no water. In keeping with hurricane preparedness, all the troughs in the fields had been filled prior to the storm. We had a lot of food and a gas stove. We were in business, and over the next few days we cooked up all the perishable food. Then our deep freezer served as a refrigerator for a few weeks with the power off. Our situation was clearly in stark contrast to what the people in New Orleans were experiencing.

Before the storm hit, the men had nailed heavy plywood over our windows. We didn't have enough plywood for all the windows, so when the Eye of the Hurricane was overhead and there was a lull in the heavy wind gusts, they ran outside and switched them to the other side!

Halfway through the storm, David ran to the barn to check the horses. The barn was solid and the horses were freaked out, but they were safe. On the following day, the sun came out and the women went to the salt water swimming pool to bathe. There was a mixture of summer camp excitement, anticipatory dread and fear of the unknown. From our vantage we could see that many neighboring fences were down and that most of the large pine trees on our property and adjacent properties were down as well. We were unable to leave the driveway since fallen telephone poles and pine trees were blocking it.

We had no real idea how devastated the infrastructure of the City was. It would take five weeks and crews from all over the United States to restore things. Our next-door neighbor, who had a lot of heavy machinery, began working with our other neighbors to move the trees.

Eventually, David and I were able to leave and drive north on a mission to find a generator. Most places were sold out of generators, batteries, fuel cans and gas. I called ahead to a Home Depot in Baton Rouge and secured one, and David, Mark, Diana and I moved into our pop-up camper so we could use the air-conditioner.

Louisiana heat is unbearable without air conditioning, especially if you have heat intolerance due to MS. At the time, I was using a walker and able to maneuver through the yard and into the camper. Diana's mother, again at eighty-five years old, was raking debris and toting water from the pond to the toilets. After a catastrophe of this proportion, we all did what was needed and did it happily.

We perceived a shift about two weeks after Hurricane Katrina. It was clear that the government was not going to help, so people organized to help one another. Neighbors went door to door and we heard stories of people who were trapped in their homes without staples. We heard inspirational stories of people coming together in service to others. Cohesion was developing out of necessity. My brother Dale arrived from Pennsylvania with supplies to help out. He and I went to the Red Cross to volunteer our resources. Dale was a trained EMT and began working at shelters.

After a few days we realized that text messages could get through and my psychotherapy group began to convene. One member mentioned that Katrina means "to purify."

We began to realize that after the initial shock and devastation, the state of Louisiana was going through a kind of purification. Crews were arriving at our door to be of service. There was a quality of open-heartedness in people that was palpable. When telephone service was restored, we received calls from all around the United States asking us what we needed. A shift toward co-creation for the survival of the collective was stimulated that August of 2005 and, due to the love so many people have for New Orleans. *An evolution of altruism spread throughout the world.*

1800 people lost their lives during Katrina. Social injustices were illuminated and half of my choir lost homes or loved ones. The devastation was heartbreaking but I feel encouraged by teachers like the Tibetan nun Pema Chodrun, who teaches about impermanence and helps us to embrace the bigger picture and a perspective that includes a loving Source. She said;

"Only to the extent that we expose ourselves over and over to annihilation can that which is indestructible in us be found."

Years in the trenches
Travels beyond
Yet somehow weathering the storm

With quick resolve
A commitment is born
With ten fingers and toes
To honor the form
Previously chosen

Never to stray
To someone else's design
Never to move
To someone else's dance

The connection is consummated
With no one consumed
A new garden planted
Fresh seeds sprouting in their innocence
Patiently
Awaiting the harvest

CHAPTER FOUR
IT AIN'T OVER TILL IT'S OVER

"The hero faces her greatest fear..." Joseph Campbell

INITIATIONS INTO DIVERSITY AND RECONCILIATION

Blog Entry: July 5, 2012

I went to secondary school at Scranton Central High School. There was a rival high school in the area called Scranton Technical High. When our football teams played, competition was fierce. I remember the cheers, "Fight! Fight! Fight!" Some players prayed to God to beat the other team. Is God listening to prayers for one team to beat another?

I grew up in a Jewish family in a Jewish community and I was sent to Hebrew school for part of the week. I studied Hebrew, where they tried to indoctrinate me into the structures from the Old Testament, but I was rebellious and 'non-compliant'. In his utter frustration, my Hebrew school principal once accused me of being a con artist. Perhaps the 'split' of being raised Jewish in a virtually atheistic home caused this conflict, or perhaps it was my willful, rebellious nature.

When I became a teenager, my family told me that I was only allowed to date Jewish boys. Was it then that the seed was planted to never marry a Jewish man? It wasn't just being told *no* that contributed to this decision, I know that from deep within my soul there was some inequity that did not sit well in my Being.

When I was fifteen I went on an eight week tour to Israel. During my travels I met many Israelis and Arabs, but I was clearly on the 'Israeli Team'. After all, I had the hair, the uniform and the cultural foundation to prove it!

When I traveled to Eilat at the southernmost tip of Israel, I had a life-changing experience, a momentary event that I've later referred to many times as a time when my consciousness shifted.

I was sitting by the edge of the Red Sea at the Gulf of Aqaba, looking through binoculars toward the Saudi Arabian peninsula. It was amazing to me that another country that was so different culturally and politically could be so close. As I explored this country through my binoculars, I had a vision of a fifteen year old Saudi girl looking right back at me through her own binoculars.

In an instant I realized that being Jewish just happened to be the 'team' I was on this time around, that I was not special nor was my team special and that I was really no different from a Saudi Arabian fifteen year old girl. This revelation blurred the boundaries of self and other, and challenged the concept of self and enemy.

When I was a freshman in high school I met a boy who I adored from the moment I met him. The fact that Michael was Jewish must have been an oversight. I boldly asked him to the Feb Sophisticate, a formal dance where girls were the initiators. After two years we were relatively exclusive. Michael was my first love. After high school however, I was somehow able to tear myself away and go to the University of Miami for college.

I can remember incidents involving Michael which were beyond my understanding. One such example was when I was meandering around the college dorm and I suddenly felt panicked and ran full speed to the elevators and to my room. The moment I ran into the room the phone was ringing and it was Michael. This didn't surprise me, because our connection was so strong.

When he and I discussed the future however, there was a disparity in our visions. We both saw us together, but he was imagining a busy urban experience while I was visualizing a quiet rural life which included many animals. In retrospect, I see that this was a fissure that could not be overcome and that our destinies would take us in opposite directions. His would take him to New York City to be a vice president of a major pharmaceutical company and mine would take me to the deep south to become a psychotherapist in and near New Orleans working with cultural diversity.

I had other experiences in my early adult life that helped to accelerate my undeniable yearning for inclusivity with diversity.

During my college years, after leaving my relatively homogeneous cultural experience in Scranton and going to Miami, I dated boys from as many different cultures as I could meet. Korean, African-American, and Japanese just to name a few. In retrospect I can see that, in part to initiate the unavoidable separation from Michael, I'd met a handsome African-American young man who would shift my worldview 180°. The feelings I had for Burgess were more than I could reconcile and once I realized that it was significant I informed Michael.

This was not well received and I paid the cost of being 'excommunicated' as a significant girlfriend in his life. In retrospect I consider these events an acceleration of my quest for a more multicultural life experience. Through my relationship with Burgess, I learned a lot about prejudice and judgment from the inside out. Although a painful process, this would give me much more insight into the complexity of intolerance. This insight carried forward into later relationships, such as my marriages.

Screenwriter Nora Efron said, *"Marriages come and go, but divorce is forever."* Some of my greatest teachings were likely acquired after my divorces and were significant contributors to the part of my life path which deals with 'reconciling conflict and diversity'.

When the well-being of my children depended, in part, on the reconciliation of ill feelings toward their biological parent, the forgiveness process became a matter of urgency.

Whether I had a predisposition for this sort of tolerance and forgiveness or whether this was part of my evolution, it clearly became a large part of my personality style. This quality would serve me well in my vocation as a psychotherapist as well as in my avocations, especially my participation in the interracial gospel choir after September

11th and in our stand against racism and sectarianism during my choir's tour in Ireland.

The concept of 'enemy' has always been a difficult idea for me to hold onto for very long. As angry as I have been at former friends, husbands, teachers or rivals, I've been unable to hold onto the concept of 'adversary' without moving into forgiveness. As much as I loved Jerusalem and my 'home team', I had equal room for the Palestinian people. I didn't know how anyone could read Queen Noor's autobiography and not feel empathy for displaced peoples no matter what team, tribe or culture they were born into.

I learned a great deal from that fifteen year old Saudi Arabian girl that day in Eilat and I suspect that she learned a great deal from me.

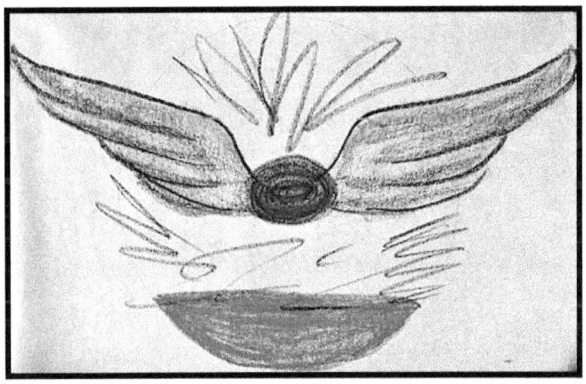

Covington Louisiana - March, 1997

Alone again
After
A brief respite

Clouds parted
Revealing
The naked

Thunder sounds
Offending the on-looker

Mirroring confusion
Becoming
Outwardly visible

And fading in the mist

WHAT EVOKES HOPE FOR HUMANITY IN YOU?

Blog Entry: July 18, 2012

When I learned that you can watch movies on your computer immediately through Netflix, I began watching documentaries like crazy. I found that when you rate the movies you view and make subsequent selections the process of subjectivity becomes much more refined. What an effective marketing plan!

In the last twenty-four hours I watched a Holocaust survivor forgive the Nazis, including Dr. Mengele who experimented on her and her identical twin in Auschwitz. I watched a boy with down's syndrome prepare for and perform his bar mitzvah with much support from his family and community. I also watched the documentary of a Palestinian girl who flirted with becoming a terrorist before sublimating those impulses. What an interesting venue for trying out different roles in life and experimenting with different evolutionary paths!

My latest selection on Netflix was the life and legacy of Werner Erhard. While watching this biography I realized how much influence he had on my life and on others who had subsequently influenced me. It is interesting how many of my former teachers have been demonized by the general public. The common denominator was that the teachings were esoteric, less mainstream and they were way ahead of their time. The context of controversy can lead to distortion by those who don't understand the teachings...*or aren't ready for change.*

When someone like Werner Erhard, who touched so many lives and lived as an example of bald-faced courage and integrity, gets taken down, it is deeply troubling to me. I suspect that he would be the first one to take responsibility for contributing to his fall, so I won't see him as a victim. Now that I think about it I believe he could have been one of many significant influences for me not feeling like a victim of this illness.

Marshall Rosenberg, Ph.D. was brought to Israel to work with Israelis and Palestinians to create a bridge for communication and resolution of conflict. Dr. Rosenberg's work is called 'nonviolent communication' or 'compassionate communication', a tool which I believe is desperately needed in our present circumstances, a tool which has the potential to spread world peace one person at a time... *one 'team' at a time.*

I think that there are many tools available to people, tools to keep us honest and expanding along the greater trajectory of our human experience. There are contractions along the way of course, healing is not linear, although at times part of me would like to believe that it is.

I believe everyone has a responsibility to move humanity forward, that the way to do this is to work with our limitations and help to bring greater awareness to the human system. In my opinion planetary changes are an external manifestation of the consciousness that has to be raised.

We look at our political system, the slowest to change in our culture, and are alarmed by what we see. I believe it reveals the intransigence of the human psyche. We all need to do our share in moving humanity forward, whether it is by watching documentaries or dramas that move us, or attending meetings that enlighten or enliven us, or by participating in other forms to which one is drawn - all in order to go beyond our present limitations.

If I am not challenged by whatever tool I choose, I will not change. I have been in a group for three years with four other people who come to my house twice a month to practice nonviolent communication. Paradoxically, these are the most psychologically violent interactions I experience. If most people, including myself, do not want to walk out at least once during the meeting we have likely not pushed our self-imposed limitations far enough!

These meetings can be raw at times, but the metaphoric container is what allows for ultimate safety. The intention of the group is to work through psychological violence and to transform this primal energy into Love. The level of violence that we as a society live with, and yet are virtually unaware of...*is astounding to me.*

Transformation occurs by recognizing that the deepest need we humans have is for connection. It is with this understanding and through a very clear technology developed by Dr. Rosenberg that we move from violence to reconciliation. Each success in our group increases the level of trust and therefore expands the human container. As our group continually practices this technology successfully, and more groups are created in the community...*I feel a growing sense of hope for humanity.*

MR. MAGOO AND OTHER SPIRITUAL TEACHERS

Blog Entry: July18,2012

It was a revelation when John, a significant spiritual teacher in my life, told me that parenting was not about making your children's lives comfortable. I probably looked at him like he had three eyes! My 'raison d'être' as a parent was not about making my children happy and comfortable?!

He explained that being a responsible conscious parent was about raising our children to be courageous, spiritual warriors, to deal with the complexities of human existence. Once again my worldview was turned inside out. As Sid described working with John, you opened your mouth and he put his hand down your throat, grabbed you by your balls and turned you inside out. Sid also has a way with words and that about describes it!

If I could pass any wisdom to my children, it would be.

"Do the absolute best you can...Love the most you are able...Forgive yourself for your limitations...and Know that it is all the way it is supposed to be."

If I could counsel myself at an earlier age in my life, I would add to the above, *We really have very little control over anything.*. However, faith has taught me that there is order in the Universe and that this order has a much better plan than I would have devised.

When Casey was young, I sometimes reminded her that she'd chosen me to be her parent! Granted, I said that when she was feeling victimized by being my daughter, so it probably wasn't the best timing but I think the message was received.

I would never have consciously chosen my parents. It certainly worked out perfectly, but I cannot take any responsibility for the perfection. Reasoning and experience tell me that there has to be a greater wisdom or, as my brothers say, "a higher power" in the Universe.

What John said that day thrust me into the bigger picture perspective of parenting. I would not have taken that leap without his urging. Then again why would we choose spiritual teachers if we could do it on our own?

It is hard for me to grasp, who are the teachers and the students in the parent-child dyad. Often as a parent I felt like one of my heroes, Mr. Magoo! While precariously venturing on in life, Mr. Magoo blindly walked forward...*and was mysteriously kept safe.*

I learned quite a bit from my children during their early years, and as they matured to adulthood that learning has accelerated. But it really doesn't matter who is learning and who is teaching. Both are a sacred and precious ritual for which to be grateful.

Whether it is through your children, a shaman or a cartoon character, being open to Life's teachings on life's terms certainly makes...*for a more interesting way to live.*

TRUTH OR SYMBOLIC STORY: HEALING BEYOND LIFETIMES

Blog Entry: July 23, 2012

Since arriving in Colorado, I've had this enormous sense of...*meaninglessness.*

Sitting in my recliner and looking at Crestone Peak, Challenger and the other Fourteeners, watching the sunrise over the mountains at 6:30 every morning and observing the monsoon winds and rain come through the desert with frequently resulting rainbows, I know that...*this is where I want to be.*

I don't question that coming back to Colorado was the right thing to do. I just don't understand how I am to *serve* with this level of disability.

Not long ago, I would often touch at least twenty people's lives during one day and I didn't question that I was making a difference. I even compulsively took care of my caregivers emotionally and their lives and their families' lives improved. Now, making a difference in someone's life feels like a rare occurrence.

Who am I if I am not impacting lives in a big way? Perhaps this is similar to how a mother feels after the last child leaves home. Is it merely an identity crisis? If so, I can do this. I have survived an 'empty nest' before. I remember the years of soul-searching and preparation. However, this time I was totally unprepared.

What I know about transformation is that you have to fall into the place where there is *no hope* and only by letting go into that state can the new way of being become manifest. This knowing is mostly mental at this point, but is growing more visceral and spiritual. I am in the place directly before the abyss, the darkness where one's greatest sense of suffering can occur. From experience, I know that this is a transitional state.

During a previous empty nest experience I coped by getting a Great Dane puppy! I moved to a horse farm, remarried and developed a whole horse community. I forgot about my son's needs at a time when he was not yet finished with high school. This has been a source of his greatest disappointment and resentment toward me. I didn't handle this empty nest transition very well.

In all fairness I should mention that it was around this time that I received the MS diagnosis. How this fits in I am not sure, but I'm sure it does.

When I was working with Stan Grof, M.D. on breathwork training, I worked on the deepest levels of my life. Dr. Grof is a psychiatrist and a prolific researcher and writer in the area of transpersonal psychology. He and his trainers travel all over the world to produce transpersonal workshops and trainings...*where I have experienced the deepest healing imaginable.*

For three years, I was a part of this training program. I traveled around the United States participating in it. During one particular training module, I awoke from a nightmare at 4:30 AM. I was crying hysterically and totally inconsolable. It was the kind of dream that felt completely real, not a dream at all.

The dream was set in Nazi Germany during the 1940s. Jordan was my son and somehow I knew that the SS soldiers were coming for us. I put Jordan in the closet and ran for safety. I suddenly realized that if I were to return to get him, I would surely be killed. If I ran forward I had a slight chance of survival.

The weight of the decision was devastating. I made the choice to go forward and simultaneously realized the enormity of my decision = to live a guilt-ridden life that would end up being marginal.

After the hysteria began to subside and I got myself reasonably together, I went to speak with Stan and recounted my dream. He felt that it was clearly a past life memory surfacing to be cleared. For people who have never had such an experience, it is important to understand the context of the training. The mere presence of Dr. Grof and his most experienced trainers created a setting for deep healing. For the less experienced with past lives, these controversial themes could be considered to be a symbolic story.

Whether this experience was a true memory or a symbolic story doesn't really matter. Even if it were a symbolic story, there was a reason for this particular story to emerge.

As a brief digression, I want to mention a very interesting book on this subject. It is called *Beyond the Ashes*, and was written by a Rabbi who started doing research into situations where people had seemingly irrational memories of the Holocaust. He found that some memories and other happenings were able to be validated by research. He posited that people were being born at this time to clear the trauma of that period in history. I should note that he was originally a cynic, and when he began to validate information and present it, he became flooded with people who had had these experiences and couldn't understand them. I should also note that a small percentage of the people with memories were in the role of a Nazi soldier.

Ever since returning to Colorado, I have been almost obsessed with watching movies with Holocaust themes. Is there a connection between the sense of meaninglessness and the imprinting of abandonment? Did I 'leave' my child before I got 'left', and was therefore handling the 'empty nest' unconsciously?

In any case, considering the level of Jordan's reactions. I'd clearly mishandled one of the most sensitive times in his life and when I consider my regrets in parenting, this is probably on the top of my list. Most parents have something they have done that they regret, perhaps to the extent where *shame* is involved. Once shame is involved, it takes a lot of personal maturity to clear the pattern.

If I were to attribute validity to Dr. Grof's interpretation of my dream at the training module, one could say that if there was an infraction of that magnitude the imprint of abandonment might recur in significant ways in my life in order for the pattern to be emotionally cleared.

Where the multiple sclerosis diagnosis fits in I am not sure. Whether this pattern informed the illness or the illness exacerbated the pattern isn't clear. What I *am* sure about at this time is that healing is happening on a level that is beyond where my mind can go at this point. And as always, forgiveness becomes a central part of the healing process...*both with other and with self.*

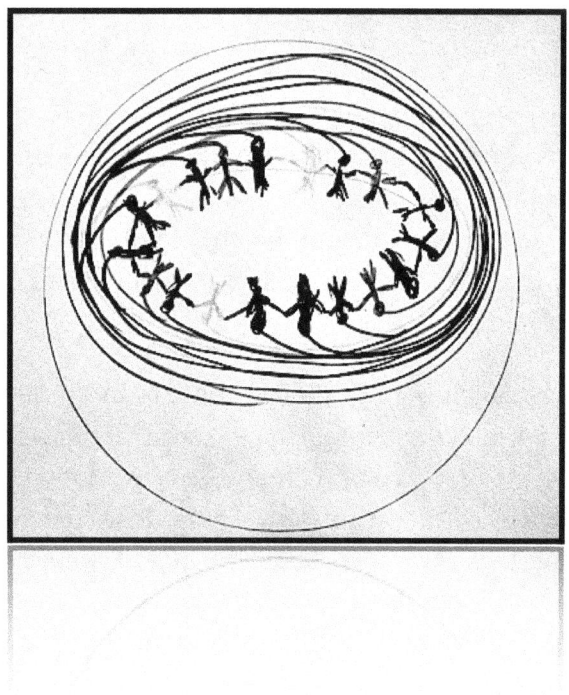

Arroyo Secco - 1996

CIVILIZATION: THE DEVELOPMENT OF COMPASSION

Blog Entry: August 3, 2012

When I was in graduate school at Tulane University in New Orleans, I had developed some pretty harsh beliefs. After studying the welfare state and seeing how some people's out-of-balance benevolence had created a kind of dependency for the less fortunate in our system I became angry. I was concurrently learning about enabling behavior and how that could cripple those who were in the role of the 'helpee'.

During my field placement at a community mental health center, I observed directly some of the unintended effects that this practice had on a few underprivileged families. I saw how a few of these families had learned to 'play the system' and how the future options of their children had become narrowed. Again I became angry. I learned in social work theory that some of the people who supported the welfare program were called 'benevolent individuals' or 'BI's', and this was not at all an endearing term.

I remember walking down Royal Street in the French Quarter once and I encountered a few crippled homeless persons.. They were asking for money and my rage at this system became channeled at them. I said, "you can get a job!", and I remember feeling righteous in response to their perplexed stares.

Everybody has seen people with extreme limitations performing Herculean tasks. How about the blind man who climbed Mount Everest? This sort of Story demonstrates the perseverance of the human spirit through adversity. In retrospect, in reaction to the aberration that seeming benevolent practice elicited. I realize that I was becoming a functional conservative politically.

At this point in my personal development, I joined intensive group psychotherapy for many years. Having been a virtual atheist and a self-proclaimed pragmatist, I began to experience empathy to a degree that I had never experienced before in my life. I had always been a sensitive, compassionate child and young adult, but there clearly was an initiation that happened when I was with that large community of people.

Perhaps it was being 'real' with vulnerabilities that helped me see that *we are all the same*...the 'old creepy man', the 'young spoiled child', the 'disabled unfortunate woman' - each of them had the same frailties and yearnings that I had in life and I came to see that all anybody really wanted was *to love and be loved and to feel connected to others.*

Seeing this was nothing short of a revelation in my life because at the same time I realized that perhaps this is what God really was. Perhaps this is what people had been experiencing, an experience which often seemed to me a reductionistic or manipulative concept. But in my being, I knew that this was my Truth. I felt an existential shift that was beyond my own personal story, it involved the story of humanity and its interconnectedness.

After this transformative experience, I revisited the issue of enabling behavior toward the disenfranchised. I noticed that *my anger was gone*. I still felt a responsibility to be judicious with generosity, but those who seemed less fortunate elicited much more compassion from me. My personal philosophy had become more politically progressive.

Now, when I try to understand the more individualistic philosophy of the conservative movement. I feel much more like what some people would call a socialist. I appreciate the development of self-sufficiency and self- reliance in one's personality but this is a lesser level of development in me.

As a teenager, becoming self-reliant was my greatest aspiration. But as I developed psychologically and spiritually, my newer goal became that of developing *interdependence with others*. This must not be confused with codependency, which can be fostered by a more limited and limiting mentality. Interdependence and 'co-creation' are both inclusive and empowering for everyone involved. They take things from an individual to a more collective perspective.

My political philosophies have transformed along with the other parts of my personality and though I recoil from polarization in any direction, the description of 'progressive' is not antithetical to my personal philosophy. But tempting as it is, I will not tread more deeply into the sticky territory of politics that is so charged at this time.

Having grown up in an affluent family, I've had more options than many of the people in my community. As I matured, I didn't understand how such inequities could be possible in a just world and I became more appreciative of the abundance that I'd been afforded.

In my group psychotherapy community, I was able to come to terms with more of the subtleties of my good fortune. As I watched my close friends struggling to afford intensive psychotherapy I developed a respect for the values they demonstrated. I felt a sense of generosity and love. I wanted to pay full price for the benefits I derived, while my friends were offered reduced rates for the same services. I was happy to contribute more since I had been afforded more. It was pretty matter-of-fact to me...*a no-brainer.*

I came to understand the tax system in America. People who have more and have had the benefit of greater opportunities can give back to the system while people who are less fortunate can derive an equalizing benefit. If one chooses to play the system, that is their karma to work out as it demonstrates a more desperate and unconscious level of awareness. Eventually, as they continue their work they will likely become more generous, or so one would hope. This is what socialism means to me.

In my Facebook profile I described myself as a 'commie pinko'. I offered this in a lighthearted way. I don't subscribe to communism! But my heartfelt desire is to do my fair share and, at times that quantity has been greater than others' 'fair shares'. Now that I am totally disabled, I appreciate the importance of disability income and medicare entitlements.

Signing up for disability was not easy for me for two reasons: firstly, I didn't want the label to limit my possibility for healing and secondly, I was not used to being the person in need. By the time I applied for disability, my disability was so advanced that the Social Security Administration didn't even contest it. In my understanding, it is always disallowed up to three times.

In the spirit of "one reaps what one sows," I like to believe that my development of generosity has allowed me to be taken care of by our federal community during my more frail years. I cannot imagine being a part of a community that would do otherwise. Civilization is supposed to be the most advanced stage of human social development and organization. I cannot imagine being a part of a civilized society at this point in my/our development...*that would not take care of its own.*

REDEMPTION: SHAWSHANK STYLE

Blog Entry: September 2, 2012

Since I've been back in Crestone, I have felt both relief and a deep layer of grief that is all too familiar. While I feel a level of vitality and well-being that I hadn't felt in Pennsylvania, there is underneath a deep sadness that is triggered by the slightest provocation.

When in the wilderness I have a deep desire to participate in life, to hike to the waterfalls, to search out wildlife and to walk my dog. But now I sit in front of my partially completed oil painting of the blue Chevy truck on the easel and wish I could complete it. In the dining room, where I sat for hours and built over a hundred pieces of jewelry, my supplies and tools sit impotently. Everywhere in my home there are reminders of my former life, which was full of robust activity and promise.

One of my favorite moments during the day is when I sit for twenty minutes in the sun in my perennial flower garden. While I sit, taking in the sun's rays, I look around at the weeds that need to be pulled. I grew up in a family where projects were cultivated and deeply satisfying. Looking around my property, I see horse stalls that are empty, tools not being used and much work that needs to get done. In the past this would excite me with the potential for creative and exciting fun to be had. Circumstances have changed.

Often when people visit me for the first time and it's been a while, they present with sadness, which I feel moved to correct. *"My life is not a tragedy"* is usually my response.

And often that is truly how I feel. This illness has required me to cultivate what is indestructible in myself. I have found a sense of determination and optimism I've never experienced before in my life and for which I am tremendously grateful.

What happens in those times when I do not feel gratitude, but feel the apparition of a life not fully lived? How do I *'be'* with this level of grief and loss without running from it? It occurs to me that there are ways of running metaphorically that don't involve my large muscles at all.

Despite my inability to complete these projects there is little sense of feeling victimized by this illness. I am grateful that I can avoid that pitfall and just deal with what is driving the compulsion to run...*to avoid the Great Grief that will often lead to an abyss.*

I am not naïve enough to think that this level of grief is merely a reaction to illness. This sense of despair predates the physical symptoms and perhaps predates my birth. I suspect it may have cultivated an environment for the symptoms to manifest and perhaps...*flourish.*

Sitting with the grief provides an opportunity to *'move toward it'*. It occurs to me that one of the teachings of this illness over the years has been to develop a certain spiritual maturity, to be able to live with discomfort to a greater degree than ever before. Perhaps I am at the precipice of another quantum leap in my development.

We always have the option to reject what is in front of us. Avoidance, however, is not a part of my repertoire these days. It occurs to me that perhaps the family projects were a way of avoiding the deeper unresolved issues that created the internal angst in the first place. This type of avoidance of feelings and the attempt to stay in an illusory sense of safety can solidify into a self-imposed imprisonment. To experience a quantum leap in development, one must be willing to venture *outside one's safety zone.*

Last night, five people came together at my home to participate in a Tibetan shamanic Journey practice. The plan for this session seemed arbitrary on the surface, but upon deeper reflection the timing was actually auspicious. Another hurricane was nearing New Orleans exactly seven years after Katrina.

As the intention for the evening became more apparent, I felt the enormous grief of the last seven years. After all, New Orleans had been my home for thirty years. I had attained adulthood there as well as raised my beloved children. After Katrina, the whole world changed for me as well as for those closest to me. Feeling transported to an earlier time allowed me to touch more deeply into this grief I had been harboring. After fifteen minutes of real-time timelessness in Journey time, I felt the lifting of a thick veil of grief that was replaced with a seemingly endless experience of joy and increased life force.

What I know from many years of working with non-ordinary states of consciousness is that this state offers an opportunity for tremendous healing to occur. Still being in a human body, it is inevitable for the grief to return, but perhaps it will return in a new way with new insights in which to experience a more profound transformation.

I feel fortunate to be able to live in a place where these opportunities are readily available on a daily basis. Whether it is a shamanic journey or an interaction with the UPS driver that transforms you, the importance is to allow oneself to be transformed...*to be transported out of the dense states of mind where one can be imprisoned indefinitely.*

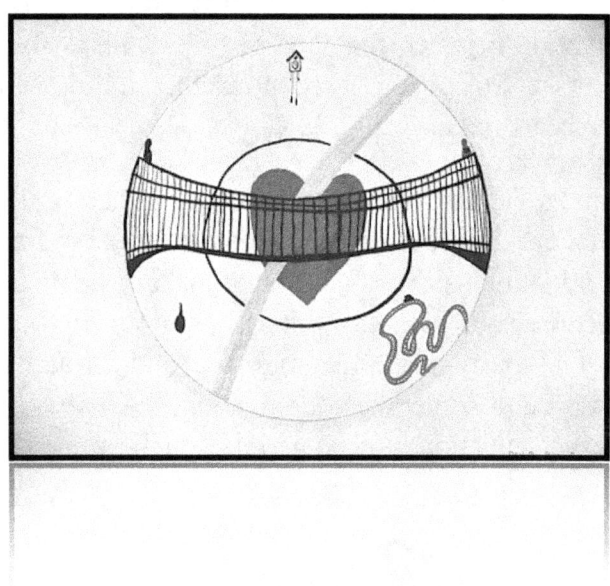

Arroyo Secco - 1996

IT AIN'T OVER TILL IT'S OVER

Blog Entry: September 10, 2012

"For what is it to die but to stand naked in the wind and to melt into the sun." - Kahlil Gibran

Boy, I'll tell you...the last year has been challenging! This has been the year of my second Saturn return which comes to everybody between the ages of fifty-eight to sixty and represents, astrologically, a second chance and possibly the last chance to...*get it right.*

It's a time to deal with any pockets of unfinished business in one's life, to finally become an elder with wisdom from the hard work of in depth self-examination. It is the time when you become your own authority, the author of your own Story. This passage is often rigorous and wrought with exhaustion and sometimes depression. And, as with most significant transitions, the outcome can be tremendously life-giving...*Mine was no exception.*

Living for decades with the symptoms of a chronic illness gives one the opportunity to explore the concept of death from every direction. In our culture, death is a concept that is mostly feared and rarely celebrated as one of life's greatest accomplishments!

Being alive at this point in history is both a tremendous challenge and an enormous opportunity for growth. As a large part of the population is aging, more and more people are moving toward that time in life where they have to consider making..."*the transition.*"

Birth is commonly seen as a celebratory event. Now it is becoming more common for the aging population to develop an appreciation for their 'final transition'. In order for one to engage in celebration of the latter, one must get right with the trajectory of one's own life experience. Why is it that in our culture death is generally seen as, at the least, disappointing and, at most...*a failure?*

There is a growing subculture that is cultivating a new, more progressive relationship with the final transition in one's life. What if, instead of it being experienced as a burden on the family when a loved one dies, the community joins with the family to celebrate this time with ceremony, prayer, and song to honor this passage in a way similar to birth, graduation and marriage?

In Crestone, we have an end-of-life program, the mission of which is to encourage individuals to create their own end-of-life rituals commensurate with their own sacred beliefs. In 1998, the community began providing green funerals and private open air cremations to support this end. The program serves as a prototype to other communities interested in transforming these experience. Here, when a loved one passes, the body is cared for in a sacred way, cleaned and anointed with sacred oils selected by the loved ones and community members. Often the body is visited in the home and a green burial or open-air cremation can be initiated if desired. Perhaps if I described my few personal experiences with this it will help elucidate the concept.

My introduction to this aspect of Crestone life occurred just before my arrival here. A beloved and respected educator in the community lost her twenty-one year old son to an apparent overdose. Along with the family, the community was devastated to hear of this loss - especially since he had appeared to be straightening out his life and was on a progressive trajectory.

The loss of this young man was felt directly, but the grief also echoed throughout the community in the form of empathy for the mother. I had not yet physically arrived in Crestone, but the grief was personally palpable. There is something about sharing that level of grief with a community that somehow makes the unthinkable more bearable. The mother was able to prepare her son's body in a sacred way, with people who loved him. She selected special hardwoods and candles and such for the funeral pyre making it a more personal sendoff.

I had been living in the community for a year when my neighbor and friend, who had been struggling with cancer for over a decade, made his transition. He, like me, had a love of animals and certain ways of doing business. After he passed on, I joined his family and our community for a heartfelt sendoff. This was my first open-air cremation and I was impressed with the content of his procession. His beloved horse and dog were included and I think you know by now, by reading my previous blogs, how I would find this appealing!

I understand that this ritual may not work for the majority of people in our culture, but most Hindus have believed for thousands of years that open air cremations are the most auspicious way to release the soul from the body. Those who feel drawn to this practice should be able to follow it. I do not wish to impose my own desires on others and at the same time but I would like my choices to be honored.

Protecting the sanctity of life is very important in our culture. In my opinion, protecting the *'sanctity of death'* should be equally as important.

There has been a lot of research on people having near-death experiences, or NDEs. While working on my masters degree in 1975, the first book on NDEs was required reading at Tulane University. It was Raymond Moody's classic, titled *Life After Life*. In 2001, the book was rewritten with Elisabeth Kubler-Ross and retitled *Life After Life: The Investigation of a Phenomenon–Survival of Bodily Death*. This book investigated over one hundred cases of people who experienced a 'clinical death' and were revived. There were striking similarities among the personal accounts revealing a state of profound peace and unconditional love.

In later years, much has been written on 'After-Death Communication'. One such classic is titled *Journey of the Souls: Case Studies of Life Between Lives*, by Michael Newton, which investigates a case study of twenty-nine people under hypnosis who describe strikingly similar accounts of their lives after death. These books and others similarly point to the fact that there is no such thing as...*death as we know it*.

Once death has been established as just one more celebratory and normal transition. Choosing life can become more of a conscious decision and the quality of that life becomes more of a...*creative opportunity*.

Having had a life-threatening illness for over ten years, and learning to live in the present moment and *to not project into a fearful future*, has given me the opportunity to explore different realms of consciousness that we will *all* experience at some point.

It is important for me to live each moment in a regenerative way and to know that when the time comes I will make 'the transition' with grace. A comforting source for this type of thinking is *Emmanuel's Book: A Manual for Living Comfortable in the Cosmos.* Emmanuel spoke to us through the author, Pat Rodeghast.

Emmanuel tells us that… *"Death is perfectly safe."*

CLARIFICATION

I want to be clear…
When I say I chose this disease, my higher self chose it for my greatest teachings.
My personality, my ego, did not choose these circumstances, nor would I ever have wanted this type of suffering.
This is an important point.
These choices are made with loving divine guidance only.
But what I offer here, in these writings…
Are tools and ways I used these circumstances to initiate deep life healing…
To flower and grow.

CHAPTER FIVE
THE VICISSITUDES OF HEALING

"The hero and newfound allies prepare for the major challenge in the Special world..." Joseph Campbell

MOVING FORWARD

Blog Entry: September 23, 2012

The greatest impulse in dealing with this progressive autoimmune illness is to stop, rest and wait for energy. Sometimes it is a loving act to rest but often it brings on more debilitation, a pattern I have only been able to see over time.

Like with the Serenity Prayer there is wisdom in knowing the difference, when to rest and when to move. One of the greatest teachings of this illness has been in the area of patience and self love. That has helped me to acquire 'body wisdom' and avoid more pronounced 'disuse atrophy'.

Then there is the discerning of the difference between disuse atrophy and the atrophy caused by nerve damage. Meandering and stumbling through these autoimmune issues is challenging. Fortunately, *my* nervous system damage seems to be more motor, less cognitive. I am also fortunate to have very little physical pain. Many of my brothers and sisters with this illness have both cognitive issues and neurogenic pain, neither of which I would wish on my greatest enemy, if I were to have one, and this leads to;

An Update Of My Protocols

I continue my daily routine of one hour in my standing frame and twenty minutes in the sun. Remember that my healing trajectory is not linear and that I've had to overcome the double fractured ankle which I sustained in Pennsylvania. I've also had to accommodate the lack of oxygen at eight thousand feet. My breathing, low blood pressure and stamina continue to improve and I was able to increase my standing time back to sixty minutes.

My primary protocol has evolved into the *Budwig Protocol*. I believe in this protocol for curing cancer and at first, I wasn't so sure that it's the best one for this progressive form of multiple sclerosis/lyme disease. But, after doing the research, I am coming to believe is that it can be tremendously helpful.

The central part of the protocol involves a daily mixture of low-fat cottage cheese and flax oil emulsified until it becomes water-soluble which is then more usable during cellular metabolism. I've noticed that, after a lifetime of chronically dry skin, my skin glows with a vibrancy that I've never had before. Since it has only been two months on the protocol I will reserve judgment, I just know that people frequently comment on my vitality these days!

As I soak in the sun's rays, I remember being told by four different healthcare practitioners for over a decade at least to practice this form of 'photon therapy'. It is interesting that it has taken until now to begin this practice consistently. Being closer to the equator makes it easier year round. And after two and a half months of being exclusively indoors, being out in wide-open spaces with the big sky of Colorado makes it...*a spiritual experience.*

After twenty-plus years of experimenting with protocols to improve my health and finding minimal improvement that registers on the physical level, but with much improvement on the mental, emotional and spiritual levels, I understand that this has been a complex undertaking. Certain states of mind have become like old friends: pregnant anticipation, discouragement, scintillating excitement, despair, and unfathomable hope. Yet through all of this I've continued to return to a baseline of acceptance and reconciliation. The whole repertoire of internal reactions has been available to me and fortunately, there has been much hope of late.

Another therapy at which I've looked at in the past has once again come to the forefront. Hyperbaric oxygen therapy has been found to be helpful with both lyme disease and multiple sclerosis. Research in the United States appears to have mixed reviews, but treatment in Europe where HBOT seems to be much more mainstream, is revealing more positive results.

While I have reason to believe that my vascular system and oxygen availability are two areas of extreme vulnerability, The *Budwig Protocol* has begun to reestablish a more effective cellular metabolism by balancing the electrical system and strengthening the mitochondria. Although I have not yet made an overall evaluation about this form of treatment, I am looking for my next step toward healing and am continually...*Moving Forward.*

WHAT DO YOU NEED AWCHIE?

Blog Entry: September 30, 2012

At the community mental health center where I worked for nearly ten years, and which provided psychotherapy to children and their families as well as providing emergency evaluations for people in crisis, I used to say facetiously to my supervisor, *"I need a 'Just Say No' workshop."*

I had a caseload of over two hundred children which included their immediate family members at any given time. This workload was way more than any one human could manage by herself. Add to that the fact that these were some of the most complicated cases in East St. Tammany Parish!

There were children at risk in the school setting, at home, with legal authorities or all three. This meant that I needed to attend meetings with many collateral organizations. There were meetings with child protective services and individualized educational planning meetings in schools as well as staffing meetings at the Youth Service Bureau and the state psychiatric hospital, all of which needed to be kept current.

I'm not sure if this is where I began to feel like Edith Bunker, running from room to room when I was summoned, but run I did! The phrase, *"your wish is my command"* became operant.

I felt a deep calling to this work and wanted to provide the most holistic, comprehensive and compassionate service possible. However, there was very little consideration of my own needs. This was a recurring theme throughout my life. Having been bred, raised and indoctrinated into the Jewish culture, I probably had '*Martyr*' ingrained into my DNA.!

A true sign of a martyr is that one's own needs are rarely considered and that consequently, the people around them always feel guilty! Whether my professional persona bled into my personal life or vice versa, I've always responded when summoned. Fortunately, I entered intensive therapy concurrent to the early developments in my career.

One of the most problematic patterns that I have seen in faltering relationships is the inability to acknowledge one's own needs. Even at nearly sixty years of age, when identifying my own needs, there are times when I have to consult a 'needs list'. This leads me to question whether there is, on a broader scale, a relationship between this underdeveloped part of the personality...*and the hatred and violence in the world.*

In working with couples who were in a great deal of pain I often presented the metaphor of two people drowning. They didn't wish ill will on the other however, in their own struggle to breathe and sustain life, they were pulling the other underwater. This is a graphic representation of what happens when one's needs are chronically neglected.

What would've happened if the deferential Edith Bunker was able to identify, acknowledge and meet her own needs in her adult life? What would've happened to Gloria and Meathead's relationship? Gloria would still be Gloria having been raised by Edith, but she would also have the imprint of Edith's empowerment. After all, when this sweet and naïve woman spoke her mind she was the wisest one in the family.

What would relationships be like with less drama? What would life be like if we attended to our own needs? What if Edith plopped herself down in Archie's chair and said, *"not right now Awchie, I'm resting."* Would the ceiling have fallen in?

Right now...*I am resting.*

Arroyo Secco, New Mexico - 1996

ASCENDANCE: WORKING WITH SOUL THEMES

Blog Entry: October 11, 2012

"We have to be willing to die to who we have been, in order to be born to who we can be." - Marianne Williamson

There are times during one's life where it becomes crystal clear that certain themes are central to one's learning curve. One major theme in my life has involved, that of *power versus powerlessness*.

When a theme recurs over and over again during critical times in one's life, the significance is undeniable. When a major and potentially chronic injury or illness is called in that can serve to bring the theme into a sharper focus, it is clear that the theme is critical to one's learning trajectory. In my opinion, when there is a teaching on that level, one is required to bring in the big guns! The urgency to integrate the teachings is registered and the intention must be unequivocal. I've witnessed this theme in every significant relationship in my life.

Such a theme can begin early and indicate an initiatory trial for one's lifetime or a core piece of work. One's birth process is significant in imprinting a person for this kind of deep undertaking and I find it hopeful that births happening now are much more empowering for the baby, the mother and the whole family.

My particular birth process involved some pretty significant challenges. I believe that during this time, births in general were fraught with a good deal of interference: general anesthesia, the casual use of Pitocin, unconscious behavior from the medical staff, the lack of emotional resources or sophistication of the parents and the like. The way I look at it, if I am here to work on power issues it is necessary to be imprinted with powerlessness. How else would I learn to overcome the challenge? The onset of the illness engendered much insight into this theme of power and powerlessness.

Many of my life's crossroads offered choices between the two options and many times I was unable to choose the former. I don't mean to portray this time in my life as tranquil, it was filled with a lot of anxiety and downright terror. During much of my early adulthood, I've felt frozen in a state of inactivity due to *the fear of moving forward*. The symptoms provided a much needed, yet unconscious catalyst to spring forward and I clearly understood that if I stayed immobilized I was going to die.

Whether this 'knowing' was overly dramatic I'm not sure, it felt literal at the time and still feels that way. In retrospect, the scope of my life needed to be much larger than what I was living. If I am to be totally objective and somewhat dispassionate regarding this illness, I am grateful for the symptoms...*the catalyst out of immobilization*. This is a clear demonstration of power (movement) out of powerlessness (immobilization).

One relatively recent example of this theme is when my last marriage dissolved. In many ways, I was overwhelmed with the circumstances of my daily life. David and I had just moved from Louisiana to Crestone and we had had an accident midway on the drive - while in my wheelchair I had fractured my femur and it required surgery. This complicated every level of my life. It affected my mobility as well as the level of caregiving required. It required more energy from David and created a lot more friction in the relationship.

When, over the months, David appeared even more overwhelmed than I did, I began to feel emotionally immobilized. I could not imagine living on my own with this illness nor could I imagine that this relationship was anything but a life partnership. As the marriage progressed toward dissolution, I became more fearful and therefore hostile. I am not proud of this, but I have learned to have compassion and to forgive myself. Perfectionism is not something I aspire to nor do I revere this self-defeating emotional state.

At one point during this excruciating process, which felt like an amputation without anesthesia. I suddenly became clear and said to David, *"if you are going to leave, then leave, you need to get out of my way because I have things I need to do."*

Where this clarity came from I don't know. At the time I remember that we were both surprised by this seeming non sequitur. In retrospect, I understand that this was coming from the part of me that was alive and well, the part of me that was already healed. It is almost as if both ego states, passivity and empowerment...*can become operant at any moment.*

As we moved closer toward separation however, only the powerless part of me seemed accessible. As was the case throughout my early life, powerlessness was the dominant pattern. An excruciating wake-up call seemed to initiate my... *'default setting'*.

Now that I am nearly sixty years of age, I can look back at these precarious passages and see that I have survived and even thrived by enjoining Sacred teachings at each juncture. It is ironic to me that at this point in my life that, while I am completely dependent on others for doing even the most insignificant daily living skills, I have more internal resources to powerfully effect my outer world and assist others than I have ever had in my life.

Perhaps attributing a 'higher meaning' to the challenges, as Viktor Frankl proposes in his book, *Man's Search for Meaning*, made the difference. Merely perceiving my challenges as 'Sacred' versus 'tragic' represents a certain triumph over adversity.

When reading his seminal book in my thirties, I could not connect with how Frankl 'framed' his devastating experience in Auschwitz. He saw his family die and did not know each day whether he would survive to see another sunset, and he framed it all as an *inspiration for accessing his life Work*. Although it is impossible to know this, exploring powerlessness must have been a soul theme in his lifetime as well. I can now understand this teaching from the inside out.

Although not everyone needs to delve as deeply into the human condition as I have, everyone has their version of these treacherous passages and profound personal victories...*Perhaps we can celebrate our triumphs together.*

Caught in the magnetic field like gravitational force
Being beckoned
Wooed by the sirens of the confinement

The lure of the walls
The walls are breathing
Seducing
Demanding total subjugation

Is it a womb
Or is it a tomb
Who are the gods
Requiring faith offered blindly

Breath takes me deeper
Into the whirlpool
Breathing
Relaxing
And spits me out at its side

THE METAPHOR OF SOCIAL MEDIA

Blog Entry: November 24, 2012

"A person isn't who they are during the last conversation you had with them - they're who they've been throughout your whole relationship." - Rainer Maria Rilke

The different relationships people have with social media are interesting to me. One can see social media, like Facebook, as a metaphor. Some people want to accrue as many friends as possible, perhaps because they need to prove something to themselves. Some people like to unfriend people as an existential statement...*"There, take that!"*

My relationship with social media varies from moment to moment. To be perfectly honest, I have experienced both scenarios described above. Perhaps our relationship to social media can be seen as...*a microcosm of life.*

Certainly, Facebook could be seen as a proverbial mirror in which to see oneself and consequently, offer a glimpse into one's sacred inner work. Does a person feel overwhelmed at the amount of time required to meet her own standards for participation? Then, how does one manage time in general? What feelings get triggered when reconnecting with people from the past? Does a person feel excited about the opportunities for connecting with others or does she want to stay separate in her own little world? One's relationship to social media can be very revealing and help point to what energy leaks may be present in one's life.

I guess social media is what you make of it. There were times when I resented my participation in the Facebook community. But lately, it has been a path of transformation and reconciliation and I've had the opportunity to be a part of a healing experience which I did not initiate but in which I cooperated. Today I feel triumphant! Healing has taken place, forgiveness has won out and I am humbled by the power of honesty and integrity.

Here is what happened. I was contacted by a former boyfriend who'd been significant in the distant past, and with whom I've had little or no contact since. He admitted to creating a drama with me in the past, a drama which had brought pain to the people most important in his life. When he admitted this to me in such an honest way, I realized that not only had I been complicit but it was one of the more hurtful scenarios I'd been involved with in my early adult life, most especially to myself. And when he brought all of this from the darkness of the past into the light of the present...*I jumped at it.*

How many of these damaging events do we have buried in the cauldron of our past experience without any conscious awareness, yet it becomes a pivotal event that engenders a great deal of self-hatred? True, it is painful to unearth and to re-experience these indiscretions, but living year-after-year in an unconscious way and building one's personality structure with a faulty cog in the foundation is, in my opinion *much more destructive.*

We then build our personalities on these false beliefs and feel a ripple of that falsity throughout our lives. We continue to believe in the illusion of our indiscretion *as a part of our identity.* To me, that is much more painful than to re-experience the indiscretion and then do the work required.

Today I am rejoicing in the revelation that I don't have to maintain a false illusion about my personality flaws throughout my entire life but can return to the time and place of the event, make it right and move on with a clearer, cleaner picture of who I am. It takes self forgiveness and one has to honestly weed through a good deal of shame to do this. Shame is the culprit that inevitably leads to self-hatred, which in turn creates a faulty foundation on which to build a healthy self-concept. The 'avoidance of feeling *shame*' is what binds the old beliefs in place and keeps individuals from the liberation of one's true self.

Who would've imagined that this level of healing can happen through...*social media as metaphor?*

META-MORPHING INTRANSIGENT BELIEFS

Blog Entry: November 4, 2012

"I want to be with those who know secret things or else alone."
- Rainer Maria Rilke

I wonder if I came into this world believing that my *'needs were too great'* or if this was a limiting belief which became imprinted early in my development. I can't remember a time when this illusory state of mind didn't seem like my reality.

I do not believe that babies come in as 'clean slates'. On the contrary, souls enter human form with much work to be done during their lifetime, with dharma to be lived out. I believe that children, before they come here, select their family members from the spirit world and that they develop their identities in relationship to these people.

Some of my opinions may be esoteric and are probably not shared by many in the general public, however there is a growing number of people who share in this belief either through a near-death experience, having had a loved one crossover, or for whatever reason the 'veil' thins and a *whole 'new world' opens up.*

Note: Former cynic, Dr. Eben Alexander, is a Harvard neurosurgeon who is on the cover of Newsweek magazine this month after contracting a rare form of bacterial meningitis and recovering from a coma. He just wrote a book about his near death experience titled, *Proof of Heaven.*

In my personal family constellation, I was the first girl after two brothers. We were three children with parents who already had way too much on their plates. As a small child I was very emotional and changeable and I suspect that this was difficult for my already overwhelmed mother. Perhaps this furthered my already existing belief...*that my needs are too much for the people around me.* With this in mind, I was fortunate that my parents had the foresight to hire a nurse for my first three years of life, a person who gave me the nurturance and consistency that I needed for my development.

In my sixtieth year on this planet I am beginning to realize that, in fact my needs are not too great! This has been quite a revelation...*Needs are just needs and nothing more.* It is the 'nothing more' that is the revelation. Everyone has needs, universal needs. My physical needs are perhaps greater than most, with the circumstances created by the illness, but my emotional needs are pretty minimal at this point. I **understand that** the 'old imprint' - *my needs are too great* - can create a 'holding pattern' in the energetic system of the body that can be likened to a traffic jam, an energy blockage which can wreak havoc in the system.

Another way of saying this is that my emotional needs are easily understood and met by myself these days. The key to this is to identify the needs and acknowledge *the beauty in them,* and then to meet them relatively effortlessly.

There is a further illustration of this development. I was in Pennsylvania recently - the place where the original belief was born - and being there seemed to have the effect of exaggerating the 'old imprint' to such a degree that it became completely conscious. Then when I returned to Colorado, where this belief is not as operant, the illusory nature of this pattern became clear and its ultimate release accomplished. My second Saturn return occurred at the end of my stay in Pennsylvania, *"the last chance to get things right!"* - perhaps this was necessary for this release to take hold. Often, prior to the release of such a deep insidious pattern, there is an intensification before it seems to burst through to completion.

Regardless of what it took for this to occur, I feel tremendously lighter and am appreciative for the purification acquired from releasing this painful recurring pattern!

Understanding one's needs in life is an important prerequisite to being able to meet them...*and therefore have a much more satisfying life.*

REBECCA

Blog Entry: December 2, 2012

"I hold this to be the highest task for a bond between two people: that each protects the solitude of the other." - Rainer Maria Rilke

My new primary caregiver is named Rebecca.

Rebecca is Lakota Sioux raised by a German family who adopted her at birth. Her 'presence' is deep and she has long dark hair and beautiful, dark penetrating eyes. Her adoptive parents named her of all names, Heidi. After what must have seemed like a lifetime of trying to be Heidi, Rebecca returned to her original birth name as she reclaimed her authenticity and her true essence.

After about twenty hours of working together, Rebecca told me, *"I wanted my work to make a difference and I manifested you...but you are better than what I had hoped to manifest."* We are off to a wonderful beginning!

A few months ago, I was summoned to a pivotal meeting with my previous caregivers who gave me sudden notice that they would be leaving after only three months of working in this capacity. Being as vulnerable as I am physically, major changes such as these can be devastating. However, one of the lessons I seem to be learning is that...*change is ultimately safe* and I felt a sense of calm along with the anxiety.

While I was in the impromptu meeting and being notified of their impending departure, I concurrently received an e-mail from Deanna, another friend and caregiver, introducing me to Rebecca. Given that this change had been spontaneous, and the fact that no one knew about it, Deanna's e-mail introducing Rebecca was completely synchronistic. That seems to be how things roll when you're in the 'zone at Crestone'!

I have an incredible team right now! Deanna had to go to Portugal for a conference for eleven days and this required many alterations to the schedule, which was a bit confusing. Last night, thirty minutes before my evening caregiver was to arrive, my modem lost its wireless signal and needed to be rebooted, which of course I cannot do myself.

Considering that my whole source of communication is through my computer via Facebook, Skype or e-mail, I figured that when my caregiver arrived she would reboot it. I waited and waited, yet nobody arrived. She had forgotten because the schedule had been so confusing. Normally I take these things in stride, but without the ability to communicate via my computer, I freaked! I saw myself sitting here in the dark all night unable to communicate and with no blankets and no food…I freaked some more.

It had been a particularly difficult week. Tuesday, five flies had attacked me for many hours while I sat there unable to defend myself and I thought I was going to go out of my mind. They continued to dive bomb my face for hours. Last night, when my modem went out, I remembered the First Alert medallion around my neck and pushed the button. I gave them cell phone numbers of caregivers to call and, much to my relief, one of my wonderful tag-team of women was able to come to fill-in *and reboot my modem!* What an experience of letting go and trusting this curriculum provides.

Another provocative incident was during the evening 'blanketing ritual'. Many Colorado nights go down to the teens this time of year, so having the right amount of cover is essential.

One evening, Deanna forgot to put my heaviest wool blanket on me during an extreme Colorado cold spell. After she'd left to go home, I called her on my computer and she said that she thought she had put it on me. In the dark I couldn't tell, but by four o'clock in the morning it would be extremely obvious because my body temperature would plummet along with the ambient temperature, so I hoped that Deanna was right. However, an hour later Rebecca, feeling that there was something urgently wrong, walked in to check on me.

Shocked to see her that late at night I remarked, *"Deanna must have called you about the blanket!"*

"No, I just had a feeling that you were needing something," she said, and sure enough the blanket was not there and I would have had a terrible night sleep.

Let me present to you...*Rebecca!*

THE VICISSITUDES OF HEALING

Blog Entry: December 13, 2012

"If your daily life seems poor, do not blame it; blame yourself that you are not poet enough to call forth its riches; for the Creator, there is no poverty." - Rainer Maria Rilke

The reactions people have when they see my physical circumstances are interesting. For example, it is not unusual for people, as they get to know me, to want to introduce me to a new healer who can 'heal' me. Just this week someone asked me whether I believed it was possible for me to heal. When people make these inquiries of me, I tend to examine their motivations.

What does healing mean to them?

Naturally, they feel compassion when they witness a challenge of this magnitude, but it is something else again when they are compelled to suggest change in my situation without really knowing me or my history. In the attempt to get their minds around the magnitude of this ordeal, I think that people project how they might feel if they were in my situation. But this time I used the questions to revisit...*what healing really means to me.*

Usually, when someone asks these questions, they are referring exclusively to the physical level of healing. I have known people with catastrophic illnesses whose bodies healed and their personalities have become more ego-driven. Of course, I also know of people who have healed physically and evolved into a blissful life with the wisdom and empathy that such a demanding teaching can bring. If healing depended exclusively on intention or determination *I would have achieved this outcome many times in the last two decades!*

The question of *whether I believed that it was possible for me to heal* is evocative since there are many layers to true healing. When asked that question this week, I responded in the affirmative, but I knew there was more to it. I knew that yes, it was totally possible for me to heal physically. Yet I also knew it was likely that I am not supposed to heal from this illness - at least not necessarily on the level on which she was thinking.

From the protocols I've been following, and the world-renowned healers I've been to on three different continents, I see that if healing was what I was supposed to do, I would be healed. If I could heal using my will, it would've been a done deal. If I could use my heart to heal me this illness would have been ancient history.

Someone who knows me and my work well once said, *"if you could heal it with love, Aliyah can do it."* I've made it a practice to turn over every stone I thought could be in the way of my healing, whether it was related to the body, mind, or spirit. I've completely changed my diet for many years at a time to accommodate the latest research to allow my immune system to normalize. Gluten, dairy, sugar and most things white were banished from my diet. Even eggs, grains, and meat were eliminated. I injected urine into my blood stream to normalize immune function. I scraped my veins to help blood flow. I flew to India for embryonic stem cells and to Brazil to see 'John of God'.

On the level of the mind and spirit I've delved, for fifteen years, into non-ordinary states of consciousness in order to identify any blocks. And when I recount all of this, I don't regret a single moment of it. All of this work has contributed collectively to what I experience as...*my healing*.

I have come to believe that if I were supposed to heal on a physical level I would have, and knowing this, I began to research other possibilities. I delved into the stories of many saints, teachers and lamas who contracted terminal illnesses and passed from this realm. Why would they attract illness to them? I came to understand that some people make an 'agreement' to take on certain challenges, including catastrophic illnesses and injuries, in their...*'pre-birth planning'*.

Terri Daniel, a hospice chaplain in Oregon, calls these people Sacred Volunteers. For many of these Volunteers, emotional and spiritual healing is a major part of the human curriculum for themselves and for others in their 'soul family' who they care deeply about. This demanding curriculum demonstrates the Sacred dharma of the archetype of *'the wounded healer.'*

For many years I believed that *my* journey was that of a wounded healer and part of the story of this archetype often includes physical healing. When the illness continued and the physical healing never happened, I came to understand that the healing must be taking place on...*an unseen level*.

Our human minds can be so *'concrete'* that we often miss the bigger picture in a situation. The misunderstanding about the end of the Mayan calendar in 2012, which many believed marked the end of the world, is another example of this 'concrete misinterpretation'. Those that believed the world would end on December 12, 2012 seemed to believe this literally and missed the possibility that a major revolutionary transition is about to occur. In my opinion, the world may be ending as we know it, but we are opening into a much greater way of...*Being in the world.* The geographical changes that are coming, the expansion of intuition and Love, will be nothing like we humans have experienced thus far.

Perhaps we can consciously expand our collective human minds to include a far greater understanding of Healing. Perhaps we can understand that people living with catastrophic challenges are not to be pitied and their circumstances feared, but they are to be celebrated as courageous spiritual warriors! Then maybe we can imagine a quantum leap into a culture devoid of illness on any level whatsoever. Perhaps we can imagine this time in history as...*the beginning of the eradication of all suffering.*

VICISSITUDES OF HEALING: ADDENDUM

Blog Entry: December 15, 2012

It occurs to me that I did not clarify something which might be significant. Despite the belief that this illness may never heal on the physical level, I am invested in remaining proactive with my ambitious protocols. The expression *"plan for the worst, hope for the best"* may be operant here.

Without fail, every morning I stand in my standing frame for one hour. Then I lay in the sun naked for twenty minutes. Vitamin D is very important for MS and Lyme disease. I juice twice a day, have a green smoothie, follow with my Budwig protocol, meditate, do range of motion work twice a day and leg massage. I added a motorized stationary bike once weekly, soon to be doubled. So I don't want to give the impression that I am being complacent, I am no slouch.

And, just to be clear, this story regarding healing can change in a moment. That is part of the *Mystery*. If I sound like *I know*, realize that no one really knows. My hypothesis regarding my healing has developed after being disappointed over and over...and over again, and after totally believing that my body would heal. If that is not going to happen, there has to be a really good reason for the alternative, and it has to be a creative, regenerative reason.

It was suggested to me by an adept channel that this illness was treating an intransigent personality trait...*willfulness*. If this is the case, what better way to spark surrender than to embark on a journey of learned helplessness, until there is...*surrender and acceptance?*

TRANSMUTATION OF VIOLENCE: A PERSONAL JOURNEY

Blog Entry: December 27, 2012

I began this blog entry weeks before the tragic events in Newtown, Connecticut occurred. After the devastation and with the country in mourning, I decided to wait for the collective angst to abate. The violence of which I am speaking in this entry is operant more on a personal level than the collective violence that has been endemic in our culture. However...*I believe that they are related.*

Working with our own internal violence is a way to do our part in meliorating the collective epidemic. If we are human, we likely have unresolved anger. Whether it shows up as outright rage, adaptive passivity or something in the middle of this continuum, we can do our share to affect the collective violence. I will now describe my own personal journey to becoming aware of and decreasing my own...*footprint of violence.*

I experienced a good deal of rage as a child. Without the ability to understand or express this anger appropriately, I would cry into my pillow at night, alone in the darkness. I suspect this is not an uncommon occurrence, as there is often much shame attached to anger. During latency, I learned to sublimate this rage. I suspect that during those years much of the anger was internalized or turned against myself. I became reckless driving automobiles, which was quite destructive, but outwardly I became passive and diffident. As I adopted the persona of a demure individual, I gave up a good deal of my *innate authentic power.*

While participating in group work with a controversial 'spiritual teacher' during early adulthood, group members were given 'shadow presents' for Christmas. The presents were specifically selected to evoke 'transformation'. Much to my horror, I was given a plastic machine gun! The nakedness I felt when I opened the present was only surpassed by the shame I felt at having this part of me exposed. If I could have disappeared at that moment, I would have. After all, this was a group of people from whom I could not hide.

This is a recurring theme in my life, where I choose people around me who do not become complicit in my denial system. Reluctantly, I took the machine gun home and over the next few weeks I learned to enjoy the sound of simulated bullets shooting out into the air. There was a feeling of suppressed power that was beginning to be released.

When I was in my 20s and 30s, I was intermittently a *victim* of violence and sometime during my 40s I became a *survivor* of violence. In my experience, sometimes a victim of violence creates a certain energetic opening that draws this kind of behavior, but this should not be confused with *blaming the victim,* because as soon as you enter into *blame* of yourself or others you re-create the undesirable behavior...*you re-create the violence.*

There is a difference between devolving into blame and acknowledging a deeper pattern that needs to be transformed. There is a great deal of violence inherent in our culture that needs to be acknowledged and transformed. Whether the imprint being transmuted by the individual is cultural or personal, violence is a pattern that needs to be detoxified within the mandala of our society, tragically so, as is revealed on an almost daily basis.

Within every case of domestic violence, I suspect that there is an imprint of the perpetrator and a related mirror image of the victim. Speaking from my own experience, I can remember the day in group therapy when I finally realized that I had been an integral part of the violence. What a revelation to see that without my complicity, the violence could not have taken place! It wasn't until I'd courageously identified this insidious pattern within me that I could finally be liberated from it. Unfortunately, the pattern needed to recur repeatedly and become more and more subtle until I was finally able to transform it.

Once I successfully eradicated the pattern in myself, I was able to more effectively teach others to liberate themselves from the violence in their lives as well as the violence endemic to our society. The metaphor I used to identify this pattern of complicity within myself and then with others was... *"waving a match near a firecracker."*

I could see the recognition in people's eyes when they were able to identify their participation in this 'unholy covenant'. This fearless awareness and the subsequent ownership of the pattern were the necessary prerequisites to the liberation that was to follow.

This revelation can hold true for sexual abuse as well. Again, I can remember the moment when I saw that only after I transcended the identity of 'victim of sexual abuse' could I be effective in helping others heal from the pattern, whether it was expressed as victim or as perpetrator!

Having experienced sexual abuse as a child, this pattern was omnipresent in my psychological work through the years until it was eradicated. It was only after I cleared the feelings of blame and anger...*otherwise the victim becomes another perpetrator* and forgave the perpetrator myself was I able to effectively work with victims of sexual abuse.

Perhaps not everyone has to clear this insidious pattern as completely as I did, but with the responsibility of working with others I clearly needed to. I have seen many healthcare professionals who have not completely healed from their pasts and they inadvertently impede the progress that their clients can make in clearing the pattern for themselves. Also it is important to realize that forgiveness is less an action to be taken than an outcome that happens once unresolved feelings are followed through to completion. *Forgiveness happens*...It is not a requirement, just an indicator that the work is complete.

Perhaps it has been the 'completion' of these forms of violence in my life that has allowed me to go beyond the perception of *being a victim of this disabling illness.* Regardless, I feel fortunate to have been able to do the transformational work and to help *'my beloved others'* on the journey. I believe everyone needs to be a part of the solution if we are to...*transmute the collective violence in our present society.*

CHAPTER SIX
DANCING WITH THE DEVIL

"The hero experiences the consequences of surviving death..." Joseph Campbell

THE TAO OF KENNY

Blog Entry: January 6, 2013

"Let life happen to you. Believe me: life is in the right, always."
- Rainer Maria Rilke

My son Jordan came to visit me last week and brought me an unexpected and somewhat auspicious present for the holidays. The unforeseen surprise was presented in a small colorful box with images upon it of characters from South Park, the animated television series that is controversial due to its adult themes. Evidently, if you choose a box from the South Park series, the character inside is a surprise. We opened it together and, lo and behold, the character was revealed to be Kenny, the orange hoodie-frocked fourth-grader from South Park, Colorado whose speech is often muffled due to constriction by his parka.

Kenny is the product of an impoverished redneck family, yet he is wise beyond his years. A recurring theme in many episodes is that Kenny gets killed in the most gruesome ways, only to reappear in the next episode with no explanation. There is little if any reference to a philosophical explanation, he just reappears as if the dismemberment of the previous episode never happened. If that isn't enough, rats frequently gnaw on his carcass!

It is hard for me to watch Kenny and not be struck by the shamanic nature of his recurring death-rebirth cycles. In Crestone, Colorado there is a strong Tibetan influence and rats gnawing on a carcass reminds me of the Sacred Tibetan teachings of the sky burial practice.

Sky burial involves careful preparation of the deceased person's body, which is then offered on a mountaintop to vultures, who are considered Dakinis or *Angels*. It is believed that Dakinis take the soul to the spirit world.

People are encouraged to witness this ritual to confront death openly and to integrate the impermanence of life. This has been a central teaching for me since Katrina, when much of my beloved city was destroyed along with my way of life. My closest male friend died within two years after he moved from New Orleans. This illness progressed steadily after Katrina and we sold the horse farm and moved to Colorado, divorced, and so on. Never had I truly understood the concept of impermanence on an experiential level until then.

It is interesting to me that of all the characters on South Park, I was gifted with Kenny. Whether the writers intend to impart a teaching about the impermanence of life while using satirical humor, to me the teaching is clearly out there, whether it is received or not.

In researching for this blog entry, I reviewed many episodes of Kenny and his cronies' adventures. In one auspicious episode, the writers considered killing Kenny off permanently. The episode involved embryonic stem cells and Kenny contracting a terminal muscular disease. During the episode Kenny died once again, and then after many episodes he finally reappeared. Is it my imagination or is this not synchronistic?

Then again....*sometimes a cartoon character is just a cartoon character.*

"SUICIDE IS PAINLESS, IT BRINGS ON MANY CHANGES" - MIKE ALTMAN

Blog Entry: January 17, 2013

"Never lose sight of the fact that every breath, every heartbeat is a gift." - Karen Timulty

"Suicide hotline fights to keep vets and troops alive."

This was the caption in today's headline news on NPR. It reminds me of an important issue that deserves discussion...*suicide.*

While suicidality as a result of trauma from war and thoughts of suicide resulting from life's confusion and stress are on a different experiential level, they share the belief that ending one's life seems...*a viable strategy.*

While professionally evaluating individuals who presented with suicidal ideation, I developed valuable assessment skills that involved asking certain questions. Did the person have the intention to die or did they just want the pain to stop? Assuming the former is the case, did they have a plan for carrying out the action?

In exploring the existence of a plan, I would explore whether they had the *means* to carry out the action. Means could involve prescription medications, various weapons or planning a particular action that would end in lethality such as driving a vehicle off the road.

All of this training in adequate assessment not only came in handy professionally, *but personally as well.* There have been times in my life that I felt so desperate that I've entertained the thought of ending my life. Fortunately, my suicidal thoughts were always in the category of...*wanting the pain to stop.* I say this because another axiom I learned on the job was that if someone *really* wanted to suicide, then there is nothing anyone can do stop them and, conversely, if they readily answered my questions it was a good sign that they were willing to *change their strategy.*

I began to see that my own suicidal thoughts came about when I let myself fall to a certain level of Despair. When I got to this point and didn't distract myself or numb myself into denial, I began to see a significant recurring pattern.

Before entering a new level of awareness, I would hit a wall of resistance. Everyone has their own particular inner *story* or monologue that gets triggered at this moment during one's emotional arc of Despair. I believe it wise to know what form this resistance takes in order to neutralize its potentially destructive effect...*and get beyond it.*

My words always seemed to be variations of, *"I just needed to die"* for the pain to stop. Granted this is dramatic, but this is not what one feels when one realizes that the toilet paper ran out or they didn't get into the school they wanted. In the moment after I made the melodramatic statement, I felt a sense of control over a situation that had felt uncontrollable prior to the utterance.

It seemed that once I verbalized the words, a release could take place and my thought process transform. After this happened repeatedly, I began to understand the pattern and I would no longer be impressed with the drama associated with...*the story*.

For many people, the inner story could involve what I think of as, *"the dark side of Hope."* This must not be confused with true hope. The former is a story one tells oneself as an attempt to *protect* oneself from experiencing the deep, excruciating level of Despair - which can be healed if met courageously. This seeming 'protection' is actually an avoidance tactic. A metaphor that demonstrates this is that of a whirlpool. If one falls into a whirlpool and struggles against the force, the person will likely become exhausted and drown. If, however, the person were to let go of the struggle, the whirlpool would simply pull them into the water and deposit them off to the side yielding a...*release from the struggle*.

I don't mean to infer that this transformational process approaches the kind of trauma the veterans and troops experience. I have worked with a few veterans and others with PTSD, and I suspect the circumstances in Iraq and Afghanistan, especially with multiple deployments, are on a level I could not even begin to imagine.

I believe our culture has an addiction to violence, as demonstrated by the reliance on war and guns for resolving conflict. With the level of military suicides exceeding the number of troops killed in combat in 2012, as reported by NPR, the causes of violence in our culture are clearly complex. I cannot help but think that when one is trained to resolve external issues through violence that one integrates that methodology for resolving internal conflict as well. Perhaps the use of violence as a strategy is what pushes a benign transformational process to the extreme. At some point the issue is no longer about making the pain stop, but about ending one's life. I cannot help but wonder what in our culture has lead to using violence as *a viable strategy.*

An interesting theory being considered lately has to do with the level of violence that gets imprinted during one's birth process. In earlier times, before births were reduced to a medical procedure, women would gather in a temple and be surrounded by loved ones. Giving birth was seen as a celebration of life. With the utilization of invasive medical interventions such as medications, circumcision and institutional settings, I cannot help but see a connection between the addiction to violence and this initiatory *imprint of violence.*

Perhaps, with our increasing collective awareness of violence on many levels, our transformational processes can be more humane. Perhaps, as the birth process becomes more about imprinting love and connection again our ways of resolving conflict will reflect those values. Perhaps we can finally, as a culture, begin to subscribe to restorative and regenerative ways of resolving conflict in ourselves and with others.

CAREGIVING–PART 1: A HOLOGRAPHIC PARADIGM

Blog Entry: February 15, 2013

"Into your darkest corner, you are safe in my love, you are protected. I am the openess you seek, I am your doorway. Come sit in the circular temple of my heart, & let yourself be calm."
- Agapi Stassinopoulos.

It might seem that anybody can be a caregiver, but in my experience...*nothing could be further from the truth*. It might also seem logical that if someone has raised a child, they could do what is required to care for another person in need. In reality, different skills and abilities are required depending on the situation, the personalities and the particular disability involved.

In my case, at the start, becoming disabled was a gradual process and the learning curve was both incremental and hard-won. I never had *'how to'* instructions and all of the basic teachings seemed to be *'on-the-job'* and in the present moment. In retrospect, much of my process was akin to redesigning the wheel and only afterwards did I discover that there was already a process in place. I'm certain it doest't have to be this way, but this was my way.

Perhaps the fact that my husband was my primary caregiver and that we were both exceedingly independent and self-sufficient contributed to this somewhat closed system of learning. One is not given an instruction manual in life, however I suspect that some people are more prepared than others, and some curricula less demanding.

Over the last decade, I have discovered that the more evolved and self-aware the individuals are, the more caregiving takes on the form of...*a holographic paradigm of care.* A hologram is a three-dimensional image where the whole is repeatedly represented in the parts. The more conscious the individuals, the greater is the potential for the development of a synergistic system - one that perpetuates love/care and self-love.

My particular learning process surrounding the vicissitudes of caregiving have been both grueling and not unlike having to place each brick, one-by-one, into a faulty foundation. My caregiver/care-recipient dyad has seemed reminiscent of the primal relationship between my mother and myself. In my experience the caregiving dyad always comes back to this primal relationship. At least this is my working theory.

When the symptoms began nearly two decades ago, I had the intuition that the overall teaching for this illness...*my soul contract* was about learning *self-love.* Early on, when I had the vision of a small child holding her hands on either side of my face with her nose two inches from mine and wanting my undivided attention, I saw that my attention had been divided and diffused. If my idea is correct, that caregiving is holographic, the entire process may be about healing the lack of self-love and seeing what is in the way for that healing to happen.

I came to see that my learning curve was to continually expand my capacity for self-love by continually expanding my capacity to let in love and nurturing from the caregiver. The caregiver's learning curve seems to be to offer caring *with as much generosity as possible.* This generosity needs to be authentic and the level of authenticity is directly related to how able the caregiver is to meet his or her own needs.

A caregiver who has not learned how to meet her needs becomes depleted, regardless of how experienced she might be. Depending on the level of need required from the person in need of care, the caregiver must have an equal capacity to provide. The more developed this relationship, the more a caregiver can become...*a Sacred provider.*

At a certain point, the illness began to progress more steadily. My husband was committed to my process in the beginning, but the requirements changed almost on a daily basis. Had I been able to see the trajectory I would have secured professional assistance. Had my husband been able to meet his own emotional needs, there might have been a different outcome. To expand our capacity to meet our own needs, we must first know what our needs are and what it feels like when they are not met. This may seem basic, but the ability to meet one's own needs is core to one's spiritual awareness and spiritual *Work*.

Had the demands of this illness been less, the learning curve might have been much less demanding. My situation however, *upped the ante* and I don't believe for one moment that this was arbitrary. I don't subscribe to the hypothesis that people are victimized by their circumstances. On the contrary, the circumstances are exactly what is required for the curriculum of the soul, whether that is understood and accepted by the ego or not.

As my awareness grew, I was able to see that my marriage was a re-creation of my primal experience with my mother.

She was overwhelmed by my emotional needs and unable to meet her own and therefore the system became one of deprivation begetting more deprivation. I do not say this with resentment or even disappointment, I believe this was the necessary design for the teaching we both needed and I have gratitude and appreciation for the work that took place between us.

That does not mean that when this unresolved primal scenario gets triggered in the here and now, that I am cool and calm. In fact, I often have to go through the same process of heartbreak, acceptance, and forgiveness which always ends in redemption and/or reconciliation. It just happens more quickly now and with more awareness, gratitude, and yes, even humor. This process was painful for both of us and it is only in retrospect that I have the full appreciation of it.

As I became more experienced in this caregiving 'yoga', the holographic nature of care and love became more apparent and concentrated. If I loved and cared for my caregivers, they would love and care for me. As my self-love grew I could see his or her self-love grow. The whole paradigm seemed to become a synergistic system of love and caring. That is when the system goes well.

This holographic paradigm of caring does not come without profound challenges. This process is far from linear and is wrought with many pitfalls and trials. More on this sacred ordeal will be covered in a later entry titled Caregiving Part 2: The Alchemy of Caregiving.

DANCING WITH THE DEVIL

Blog Entry: **February 18, 2013**

"For one human being to love another; that is perhaps the most difficult of all our tasks, the ultimate, the last test and proof, the work for which all other word is but preparation." - Rainer Maria Rilke

When I was about to turn forty, I had been married and divorced twice and lived with my two children in a beautiful turn-of-the-century Louisiana home on the Tchefuncte River.

I had been employed at a community mental health center for many years, working toward my state license as a psychotherapist so that I could start a private practice. I lived in a beautiful artist community and had many friends. My heart was healing from the devastation of my marriages, and I was continuing to learn who I was.

I was becoming increasingly aware of a deficit in this area of my life. From childhood onwards I had no idea who I was, I had no idea of my own value. I'm sure this baffled my family and the people who loved me. This was an area of deep inner work that I never could seem to enter into.

My mentor of the past decade and my closest friends could not understand the choices I'd made, which reflected low self-esteem and a level of self- destruction. I saw the effects of my choices in my children and felt grief regarding this but I had little understanding of how to change the pattern. I saw that becoming more aware of this confusion inside of me had the potential to bring more insight and compassion into my work with others. I knew that there was a connection that could bring healing to my limited sense of *self*. I just had no clue how to effect that change.

I had a picture on the wall of my psychotherapy office that showed two alternative paths. One was straight and direct and the other wandered dramatically. The point was that neither path was right nor wrong, It was a matter of individual choice. I came to understand and then teach that for some people the meandering path was the necessary one, otherwise the benefits of more complex teachings would not be realized. It was not easy or more expeditious, but it was the necessary path for some.

My clinical strengths were working with children, adolescents and their families as well as women's issues and working with couples, but it had become clear to me that there was a glaring deficit in my professional development, luckily I was open to learning from my clients.

One afternoon I worked with an adolescent girl and she showed me her artwork. She'd drawn a yin-yang figure and explained the meaning as, *"there is dark in the light and light in the dark"*. I was struck by the wisdom of her interpretation of this perennial truth. I saw that I was gifted in seeing the light in the dark, but was limited in seeing the dark in the light and in the clinic where I had been employed for many years both skills were required. The clinic had treated the likes of Robert Willie, the inspiration for Sean Penn's role in the movie *Dead Man Walking* - the man who had murdered many teenagers in Louisiana. A decade before my presence there, Willie had sat in the waiting room in chains...*waiting to be seen.*

One day a week we clinicians were required to see walk-ins. These were people requiring evaluations for medication or hospitalization. I could trust my judgment 99% of the time, but on a few occasions I underestimated the depth of malevolence and the destructiveness of the sociopath.

On one such occasion I was evaluating a parolee who was a sex offender with multiple offenses. A typical evaluation of this sort would take approximately fifty minutes. After two hours I found myself captivated by the fascinating stories this ex-convict and sex offender was spinning. I was snapped out of the trance when he saw my young teenage daughter's photograph on my desk and made a sexually provocative comment. I immediately transferred him to the psychiatrist and realized how badly I had just...*been 'played'.*

It was then that I met Jamie. Jamie was a gifted case manager at the clinic whose job was to deal with cases that were referred to him by myself and the other clinicians. He had an uncanny ability to connect with clients and I could see that his work would reinforce and forward my own work with them. In my heart, I felt my job was to teach people to see and experience their own lovability. There was a quality in Jamie that was profoundly effective in this area well beyond his twenty-five years. I can see now that I was drawn to this quality like a moth to the light. We developed a partnership in working with my clients that afforded growth and intimacy. Over many months I found myself *'falling into'* the most unconventional relationship of my life.

Paradoxically, I experienced profound love mixed with what I can only describe as frustration and confusion. During the times marked with frustration, I would find myself slipping into self-doubt and self-loathing, the depth of which I had never experienced before in my life.

This was a time in my life in which I was exploring my creativity. After having written poetry for many months, I presented my work at my first poetry reading. It was a recurring pattern that as I became empowered with self-expression I would sabotage myself with a romantic relationship. This was a quality that saddened and confused the people who loved me the most. I could see the confusion in my friends, but I was unable to grasp the significance of this recurring and insidious pattern much less see how to change it.

The unconventional nature of my relationship with Jamie drew criticism. With a fifteen-year age difference, I constantly found myself defending its validity. My closest friends were supportive, because they trusted my tendency to learn from all of my experiences.

This controversial relationship with Jamie involved personal connections with his family members which I found extremely satisfying. They were wonderful people and loved me and my children. We would go camping together, build fires and play music. As we hiked in the woods, his father would identify and teach me about the plants and trees growing in nature. After the pain and oppression of two divorces, it was liberating to once again be able to experience the simplicity of life. On one level, this seemed to be just what I needed.

There was however, a dark side to Jamie, who had a biographical history of parental abandonment and alcoholism. He had violent night terrors, like none I had ever seen. He would wake up screaming and drag us both out of bed, certain that he and I were being killed. Over time he became increasingly more volatile and I began to fear that I might be in physical danger. Being a psychotherapist, I was also intrigued by this behavior and on a visit with his mother I witnessed the most profound relational reconciliation of past alcoholism that I had ever experienced in my life thus far.

The extremes in my relationship with Jamie were both deeply satisfying and profoundly troubling. As the relationship progressed, the emotional extremes became more exaggerated. My own level of self- hatred was almost violent, although it was internalized. **Even with all of this, I carried through with the relationship and even had hope of it progressing in a more positive direction.** One day however, one of my beloved female clients came to her session and reluctantly disclosed not only a profound lapse of judgment on Jamie's part but a deep personal betrayal and professional breach of ethics I could never have imagined in my wildest dreams. Evidentially, when I was on a spiritual retreat in New Mexico, Jamie had entered into an inappropriate relationship with the mother of adolescent boys I had entrusted to his care. This behavior had left the family in emotional shambles.

When I confronted Jamie with this behavior, not only did he deny the accusation vehemently but his denial came from a place of such seeming authenticity and reverse outrage that I really didn't know who to believe. The shame and self-hatred was almost more then I could bear. The effect on my clients was the antithesis of what I worked for. My world crashed down. Not only was my personal life in shambles, but my children and clients were effected by the bad decisions I had made.

This created a time in my life of introspection which led to a profound existential shift. I had hit bottom, which led to a life-changing decision to withdraw from all romantic relationships. This catastrophic experience had gotten my attention and I was unwilling to go forward in the same way that I had been. There was too much devastation and I was the common denominator.

At this point in my life, I entered into something I had avoided for many years. I entered into a deeper and much more profound relationship...*with myself.* Initially I was terrified, I didn't know what of but the fear of repeating this hurtful behavior was greater than the fear of the unknown. At forty-two, I turned around and faced myself for the first time.

After the initial anxiety and resistance abated, I began to know myself for the first time. I not only felt liberated, but I was finally becoming completely comfortable with myself. Not only had I connected with a deep love of self that I'd never been able to access, but the blind spot regarding gradations of the spectrum of sociopathy was profoundly transformed.

THE PATH OF THE WOUNDED HEALER

Blog Entry: April 7, 2013

"The purpose of life is to be defeated by greater and greater things." - Rainer Maria Rilke

If we are alive and having this human experience, I believe we have made a personal choice to do so. In his best-selling book, *Your Soul's Plan*, Robert Schwartz asserts that for every soul on earth there are two others wanting to come into the body.

Being in body must mean we were the ones who were selected, however that selection process happens.

If this idea is true, each of us must have important work to do. When we have completed the work of this lifetime, then we no longer need to be in our bodies - the temporary vehicle for our work. We can return Home to the Spirit world where we are met with previously deceased loved ones patiently awaiting our return.

In our culture, there is an endemic fear of death that is unfortunate, as this fear causes much suffering. After all, everybody will cross over at some point as everyone before us has. Everything I have read about people who have clinically died and returned portrays a beautiful journey enveloped in a profound state of love.

Why would one's departure after a long, well-lived life or a prolonged illness elicit anything but a celebratory reaction from loved ones left behind? It is understandable to me that there would be a significant grieving process when losing a loved one, especially if that life has been tragically cut short by illness or traumatic injury. However, I have also witnessed Herculean efforts by the medical community to keep individuals in their body no matter what level of suffering they might be going through.

Being in one's body can be a demanding and often arduous experience and for some the fear of transitioning may be a practical strategy for staying in one's body through life's profound challenges. During a protracted illness, however, the stages of death and dying can lead to an acceptance of one's mortality, the journey may be completed more quickly by the person dying while the loved ones they leave behind are still in an earlier stage. Cultures that understand the immortality of the soul tend to be more...*celebratory upon one's crossing.*

The decision to leave can happen in a split second or it can happen over time. I believe that the soul contemplates and designs the plan for one's lifetime while in the Spirit world, carefully choosing when to enter, where to enter and with whom to enter as well as when and how to leave. Alterations can be made along the way depending upon choices we make, but basically I believe the general design has been carefully selected with much awareness and with much beloved guidance.

There have been two different times in my life that I can recall where I had to consciously choose to stay in my body despite overwhelming circumstances that were unfolding. In my late thirties, when the neurological symptoms began, I had an overwhelming premonition of what was to come. Whether it was a true recollection of some *previous* choice, bald-faced fear at what was to come or both, I went through one of the most difficult periods of my life.

I remember lying on the sofa, unmoving while watching the clock change over a three-day period. My children were young and I felt very torn about giving in to this profound *contraction*, however I felt that I had no other option. Fortunately, my husband was very understanding and picked up the slack, giving me time to process this seemingly catastrophic passage. After a few days, I pulled myself up with whatever courage I could muster *and re-entered my life*.

My commitment to my children helped me find the courage to move forward. During this period I lost forty pounds and desperately sought out whatever help I could get along the way *to keep moving*. I found a healer in Tylertown, Mississippi, to whom I would drive weekly for sometimes four hours sessions and where I began to explore every aspect of my life. I remember the day she noticed my excessive weight loss and brought me carob soy milk to drink, which felt like mother's milk. From that moment on, I made the choice to stay the course no matter what would be required. This choice was made on a visceral level and only became conscious in retrospect.

As seemed to be the case with many of my life's more profound teachings, I was called to use what I had learned in my role as a psychotherapist who has led hundreds of *'travelers through the wilderness'*. At that time, the father of my daughter's girlfriend committed suicide in the most violent way imaginable leaving his family in emotional shambles. His wife, who had become my friend, was in shock and began losing enough weight that it became life-threatening. I could see the level of despair she found herself in and the resulting life/death choice that was in front of her.

Because of my own recent experience of being in that liminal state *and having come through to the other side,* I could recognize the choice she had in front of her. I could speak to her with confidence and empathy about this precarious passage in her life which gave her the freedom to fully be in this vulnerable place *consciously.* By feeling less isolated in her despair and hearing how I had navigated through that place, she was more able to find her way back.

I felt grateful for having successfully returned and to be able to help a family that I cared about. Not unlike Viktor Frankl's teaching to attribute greater meaning to one's suffering, I felt gratitude to have been of service and I was able to find meaning in my suffering. This path can also be understood as the archetype of the wounded healer, *a shamanic journey* where the healer travels through the underworld in a journey of physical or emotional illness and then heals and returns to help others find their way.

The second experience where I felt that I had to deliberately choose to stay in my body was when I was sent to a nursing home for ten days to receive IV antibiotics in 2012. I was unprepared for the level of despair I felt from the other occupants *and* for the level of despair I felt from the staff.

Being hypersensitive to my environment, I have to be careful where I allow myself to go. Attention to diet is a vital part of my daily protocol, which is designed to support the mitochondria (the building blocks of life) of my cells. The processed food in this facility, hot dogs, baloney and tater tots, was completely unpalatable and unacceptable. Fortunately, my family and caregivers brought me food on a daily basis without which I would have again had major weight loss. With the support of my family, I chose to stay.

There is an understanding that, *"If you are wondering whether your work of the lifetime is complete, if you are still in your body, it is not."* This brings to mind the question of *where* this choice is made. What part of us is asking the question and what part of us is doing the answering? These *'choices'* are made in concert with our higher selves, which are intricately connected with our guides, teachers and the Masters...*Nothing is arbitrary.* It is all a 'Sacred adventure' designed to elicit our Soul's evolution.

It is not our egos or our lower selves making these decisions. These are courageous decisions made with much consideration of the trajectory...*that will lead to our soul's greatest level of growth.* From this perspective, many of life's choices have a greater meaning and we understand that some of life's complexities can only be left to the *Mystery.* Understanding the intricacies and challenges of being in a physical body makes choosing life *a courageous and heroic journey.*

ENCOUNTERING SHADOW: A RISKY PERSONAL DISCLOSURE

Blog Entry: **April 16, 2013**

"The future enters into us, in order to transform itself in us, long before it happens." - Rainer Maria Rilke

It has been pointed out to me on a few occasions lately that *I can be 'difficult'!* The 'vicissitudes of difficulty' usually have to do with those around me feeling slighted. At these times I have been described as *condescending, disgusted* and other variations of this theme.

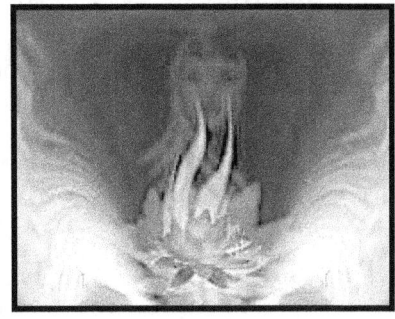

What is particularly interesting to me is that my internal experience is totally different than the other person's perception. Depending on how safe I feel within myself or with the other, this excruciating provocation could be talked through, or it could involve a premature dissolution of the relationship depending on how the challenge is met. It occurs to me that this kind of incongruence can be happening all the time and I thought I would explore, dismantle and share about it. As I teach something, I integrate it more deeply into my own Work...*Thank you for being a Witness to my process.*

Initially, when confronted with this pattern, I felt a sense of liberation, both because I instantly recognized the source of this projection as well as how to transform it. I clearly remember being on the receiving end of this *'expression'*, as my mother demonstrated this unconscious pattern frequently. There is a book that has recently come into circulation that was written by a comedian, the title of which says it all, *If It Isn't One Thing, It's My Mother.* This title expresses so well the primal relationship with one's biological mother and the liberation that comes from resolving the issues that come up in this relationship.

As I began to delve into this pattern, I bumped into a certain level of shame. Shame is usually the culprit when one meets an unconscious pattern that has been repeatedly problematic in relationships. The fact that I have caused other people's suffering as well my own elicited much sadness. Once I felt the sadness, I was able to move into a state of empathy. Empathy is the antidote to negative states of mind as well as the likely outcome once more difficult feelings are felt. I don't mean to imply that reaching empathy is an easy process, it takes a good deal of internal work and maturity to reach this state. The process can be complicated if one has the pattern of becoming defensive. Defensiveness usually shows up as an anger reaction that is a manifestation of resistance. The common pitfall almost always has to do with shame being present. Once shame has been identified and felt fully, healing can proceed.

I'm fortunate to have done enough work on myself to not succumb to this insidious complication very easily. That doesn't mean that in my quiet moments with myself I don't struggle with a level of self-hatred but fortunately I am able to work through that privately, so that the interpersonal relationship doesn't become impeded in the moment. My goal is to spend less time in this state of self-hatred than before and I notice that this intention is manifesting in my practice.

Much of the conflict that shows up in interpersonal relationships needs to be worked out internally. Knowing one's own *'triggers'* is vitally important and shadow work is essential in understanding the pitfalls that are sure to befall all intimate relationships.

My 'triggers' often have to do with becoming afraid. I've covered this frequently in my past blog entries, fear has been a trusty traveler during my long journey toward healing and is usually the culprit in most of my relational breakdowns.

I went through many years of...*being afraid of my fear.* In our culture, fear is demonized. I suspect it is demonized because fear is a part of the collective human shadow and when it is unconscious *fear is often met with more fear.*

In physical therapy the other day, when being transferred to my stationary bicycle, I had a revelation. I shared with Harald a significant insight the depth of which surprised me. I asked him to remember a game we probably all played earlier in life, where one person would stand in front of another and fall backwards in total trust and the other would catch him or her. Harald remembered doing this with an expression of joy mixed with trepidation on his face. I told him that this is what my life is like on a minute-to-minute basis. It occurs to me that this sort of life curriculum can only be necessary when mastering a significant feeling like *fear.* Situations like these are when I feel tremendous gratitude for my particular process.

During my marriage ceremony in 2004 my friend Alexandria proclaimed, *"Aliyah's life has always been about transformation."* I didn't realize how true this was at the time. Most of my adult life has been spent being a student or a teacher, and often both at the same time. I feel so much gratitude in my heart for the wise people in my life: my friends, my children and the caregivers. Each encounter allows me to practice this Sacred process of intimacy that never ceases to take me to my depths...*and which makes it possible for me to reach my heights.*

Arroyo Secco, New Mexico - 1995

SPRINGTIME IN THE ROCKIES

Blog Entry: May 22, 2013

"Everything is blossoming most recklessly; if it were voices instead of colors, there would be an unbelievable shrieking into the heart of the night." - Rainer Maria Rilke

Coexisting with a chronic illness that is both degenerative and progressive, I have had to acclimate to *being* with a continual loss of *functioning*. Almost like drinking water, mourning the losses has been an essential part of my process.

In order to move forward in life however, focusing on what is operative *has been crucial.*

When I was able bodied, I can remember when riding my bicycle a large rock appeared on the road in front of me, my focus was intently on the rock and running over it was unavoidable. I had to train myself to see the rock and focus elsewhere to avoid the certain collision. With this chronic illness, I seem to have to execute the same practice - to move forward and not focus on the intractable symptoms in my field of vision.

It has taken much work to become confident that my attitude is positive and regenerative. I meet many people with chronic illnesses who have not done this work and it can be painful to watch the suffering. I have compassion and remember my suffering in the beginning.

As we age in our culture, acceptance of our limitations is unavoidable. As we live longer, the illnesses and accidents become issues to shape our character. We can see them as *helpers* along the way. I believe we are here to build character, develop our hearts, and learn to love better. This reminds me of an old Hasidic saying, *"on our deathbed, one never says, I should have worked more."* The measure seems to be...*how well were you able to love.*

It is springtime in the desert at 8000 feet. The streams are flowing abundantly with rainwater and the trees are pregnant with new buds. After the quiescence of winter, springtime enters with a certain euphoria in the Rockies. The paradox of the flaming red blossoms on the cacti and the tender yet tenacious sprouts pushing through cracks in concrete remind me of the perseverance and persistence of life. The gradual renewal in the air offers me, both humbly and vociferously, yet another year on the planet. With much gratitude and mindfulness of what has been offered...*I accept the generous proposition.*

CHAPTER SEVEN
TAKING THE LEAP:
THE BODY AS MESSENGER

"By the hero's action, the polarities that were in conflict at the beginning are finally resolved..."
Joseph Campbell

GENERATIONAL HEALING THROUGH THE RITUAL OF BIRTH

Blog Entry: May 28, 2013

"You must have chaos in you to give birth to a dancing star."
– Frederick Wilhelm Nietzsche

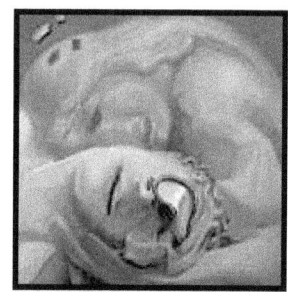

When I was twenty-six years old I became pregnant for the first time. Before this, growing up was for me, a fearful endeavor and becoming pregnant was assuredly *grown-up!*

I didn't know then that I indeed had what it took to meet the challenges of my Sacred Transitions in life to such a degree. In fact, well before my first pregnancy and around the time of my graduation from graduate school, I was literally bleeding internally from the terror of being on my own.

After inconclusive medical testing it was determined that the worrisome physical symptoms were psychosomatic. Psychosomatic does not imply that they did not exist. The blood was real and the pain in my gut was real. What was even more *absolute* however, was the terror that I would not be able to secure a job and support myself. Where this profound lack of confidence came from is a mystery to me but it was clearly a challenge that needed healing.

Without the maturity of healthy coping skills, I grabbed onto the closest support, support that I believed would be lifesaving. Making choices from fear never ends well and it is with humility and compassion for myself that, after much inner examination I am able to acknowledge that this is how I chose my first husband.

From the vantage point of *now* I can see the recurring pattern as and abject lack of self-confidence and the fantasy that 'the answer' lies somewhere outside of myself. If I had been given an instruction manual upon taking birth, it would have stated, *"Warning! Relying primarily on others can be dangerous for your development!"* In retrospect, it seems that these integral teachings were *the core of my soul curriculum on this physical plane.* Ironically, once this knowing is understood and accepted, there can be ever increasing joy and gratitude surrounding the navigation and ultimate integration of these teachings. This was true for me then and is certainly true for me now.

Once I secured my first professional job and as I began to develop my professional persona, the anxiety and physical symptoms completely subsided. Another recurring pattern, *the unfounded certainty that I would fail,* was replaced with a sense of accomplishment and accolades for the level of responsibility and proficiency I was able to acquire.

When I became pregnant, I was ecstatic - it was as if this was the moment I was born for. I had continuous internal communication with my perinatal inhabitant that I was yet to know. The pregnancy proceeded with much joy and amazement. My marriage however, was not supportive - it was contentious and deeply disappointing. Another warning from the instruction manual would read, *"Decisions made from fear will bring disruption and suffering!"* In retrospect, I understand that the chaos of this marriage would eventually lead to a new order of understanding, but in the trenches it was difficult.

We were committed to natural childbirth and started Lamaze class on schedule. I'd prepared my body with daily prenatal yoga and stretching exercises. When it came time to practice Lamaze breathing together however, my husband was extremely resistant and I didn't have the communication skills I needed as yet. I felt alone and imagined a painful childbirth with no support.

Finding myself alone and helpless was always my greatest fear in life and as the fear of experiencing childbirth alone accelerated, I went to my obstetrician and asked for a cesarean. Of course he was more than happy to oblige.

The cesarean set in motion a series of events that created much suffering, *as making decisions from fear always does*. On the other hand, birthing and parenting my daughter increased my level of confidence. Within a year I found a therapeutic community where I could begin to face my deepest fears and I now had the support to leave my marriage which had become increasingly abusive and included alcoholism. Little did I know that facing my fears would be a lifetime endeavor, however this time in my life provided the pre-requisite knowledge and experience to adequately move forward with confidence.

Six years later, when faced with a second marriage and a second pregnancy, I was not given the choice for natural childbirth by the obstetrician - during those days natural childbirth after a cesarean was greatly discouraged.

However, this time I was sure to have my husband by my side. I was not alone and helpless and I had local anesthesia exclusively, instead of a local and a delayed general.

Jordan was born and I spoke to him, his initial crying ceased instantly as he looked at me with recognition. Despite the birth process being a medical procedure, I felt more empowered with my choices. It was not the natural birth that I yearned for, but there was much connection and bonding. I suspect that I'd chipped away at the belief that in all major transitions I would be alone and helpless.

Thirty years later, Casey was experiencing her first pregnancy and she had begun to express anger and resentment toward me. At the time, I had the fortuitous opportunity to be working with a practicing midwife as a caregiver. She lovingly and wisely informed me that this was a natural and necessary part of the healing of Casey's own birth trauma. She needed to clear the way for a more empowered birth.

With that information I was able to be totally present and compassionate for my daughter. With the tutelage of my friend the midwife, I came to understand that birthing was an opportunity *for accelerated healing.*. As the conflict resolved, Casey shared her process with me and, as was often the case while watching her process, I was in awe of her courage and her grace.

While she was preparing for childbirth, Casey sent me a link to the documentary, *The Business of Being Born*. This classic documentary criticizes the view of contemporary childbirth as a medical emergency requiring medical intervention as opposed to a natural occurrence. While watching the documentary I was mesmerized by the profound level of support that was available to women. Sadly, this level of support was never there during my birthing years.

Another profound revelation that occurred to me while watching this documentary was that I could feel the considerable amount of healing I had done since I had given birth. Becoming increasingly aware of the courage that I had accrued while living through and with this illness, I revisited all of the medical procedures I had bravely entered into on three continents. While watching this documentary, I was able to see how much support from others I had been able to let in over the years and that I no longer felt alone and helpless, *I finally realized that I could do this.*

I saw that I finally had the courage to give birth naturally, and that *"I had what it takes!"*. When I realized this I felt a profound internal shift of empowerment. I shared my revelation with my daughter, not completely understanding the significance, but trusting that there was much. A few months later Casey gave birth to River with no chemicals, no medical intervention and a loving husband by her side. I cannot know whether there was an impact from my internal work, but I have respect for the unseen realm and I feel it necessary and a privilege...*to do my part.*

Falling into myself
Like slipping
Into the ocean

Submerged
Finding new life

Wondrous
Colorful
Fragments of Truth

Moving
Dancing
To find a rhythm
More truly my own

LEADING FROM VULNERABILITY: A PARADIGM SHIFT

Blog Entry: June 20, 2013

My early years were spent floating, metaphorically. I moved as the currents seemed to arbitrarily move me. I like to think that I was acquiring information and strengthening my foundation, *I'm sure there is truth to that.* In graduate school when I began providing psychotherapy treatment to others, I realized that I was in over my head, on the emotional level.

It was then that I entered psychotherapy, to begin to make sense of my history, my present life and to develop any gifts that I might have in this area.

This trend toward self-exploration can be likened to *'taking a moral inventory'* (or the fourth step in the 12 step program). At this point, everything became a means toward increasing my self-awareness, learning more about who I was and what I was to bring to the world.

I now begin my sixth decade in this body and certain self-defeating and recurring patterns are becoming clearer *a necessary prerequisite for healing.* I had an overactive 'will center' in childhood and my tendency through life has been to push forward regardless of any resistance that I might encounter. This 'blind persistence' is a quality revered in our culture, however on a more subtle level it can create a significant imbalance and I believe that much of my work in this lifetime was to bring this self-defeating trait into balance.

Prior to the beginning of my physical symptoms, I lived this pattern of willfulness unconsciously, like floating in a rudderless boat. Once the symptoms began, I became more aware of the imbalance. My past actions seemed to emulate the pattern of moving two steps forward and three steps back. It seemed that each time I had a breakthrough, there was a resulting backslide. As many insidious unconscious patterns do, it became more exaggerated and therefore more apparent as time went on. As I became more aware of the suffering this pattern caused, I suspected that it was triggered by a sense of unworthiness but just knowing that did not change the pattern.

In 2010, when I went to India for embryonic stem cell treatment, I hoped to face the obstacle to my recovery head on and, through the dramatic healing described in an earlier blog entry, I began to strengthen on all levels. Three months later when I returned to India for more treatment Basha, my beloved Great Dane, tragically died and this heartbreak was too great for me to..."*grab hold of myself.*" Despite seeing the pattern, I felt powerless to alter the trajectory of the contraction. I know that healing is not linear, but once a recurring pattern becomes conscious, the way to move through this wall can become clearer. Still, I began to lose ground once again.

Returning to Colorado in 2012 felt like a renaissance of sorts. I'd become so debilitated in Pennsylvania that I seriously questioned whether I would survive another move, especially one to 8000 feet altitude when I had significantly diminished respiration. However, being faced with a living situation that was neither supportive nor regenerative, I had to choose between the *the familiar and safe* or moving into the unknown. In the past, the anxiety caused by such a move would in and of itself cause a backslide. In spite of the anxiety created by this change, I gathered my inner resources and moved forward no matter what.

Crestone can be a magical place if one wants to undergo serious inner work. If one is in the right place emotionally, the energies will align and *'push the work'* whether one likes it or not. My closest friends and I clearly like it. I am ready for the next passage along my journey. To say it another way, I am existentially saying… *Yes.*

Having been a competitive athlete most of my life, I believed from a young age that my value was tied up in winning. I swam, ran, and competed like my life depended on it. This ability along with my willfulness created what the Buddhists would call a 'fixed identity', an 'insidious pattern' or *"how one tries to put solid ground under one's feet in an ever shifting world."*

The last month in Crestone has presented the most anxiety provoking time since I have returned. Changes in primary caregiving and the conflict that ensues would have sent me into a significant backslide. However, in the last two weeks I have consecutively broken my speed record on the stationary bike! I also continue to improve in many other areas. I cannot remember a time where I voluntarily entered the place of *'not knowing'* and did not shut down physically and emotionally.

However, it seems that even in Crestone *healing is never simple.* It's as if the Universe tweaks you to be sure the teaching is enduring. Last week my transverse arch, an area of ligaments that hold the metatarsals together, separated and painfully collapsed resulting in a chronic torn ligament. I felt discouraged, in the past this disappointment would have created a significant setback. My mind would have created an impervious sense of failure. The self-hatred that would have been generated by my heartless reaction to physical vulnerability would override any sense of empathy around the injury, which would exacerbate it. This may be a pattern that led to the progression of physical symptoms.

My wise friend Judith challenged me this week when she asked me, *"Can you move forward, leading with the collapsed foot?"* This question stimulated an existential shift. Can I allow my vulnerability to lead the show rather than my arrogance and the fixed identity of the ego? In that moment I understood the wisdom of my physical vulnerabilities. In Byron Katie's book, *Loving What Is*, she states, *"When I am perfectly clear, what is... is what I want."* Her work is wonderful practice for...*acceptance.*

While I am becoming comfortable with vulnerability, both mine and other's, I appreciate the gifts the physical symptoms offer and my willingness to do whatever it takes to...*Love What Is.*

LET GO, LET GOD: WALKING MY TALK

Blog Entry: August 8, 2013

"Good or bad, happy or sad, all thoughts vanish into emptiness like the imprint of a bird in the sky." – Chögyam Trungpa

There is a certain lightness that is required when I formulate my thoughts around a new blog entry. But this past month has been anything but light as there has been much change in my daily life. Although I entered into change consciously and willingly, the anxiety that ensued was breathtaking.

The result is that this has been the longest lapse of time between blog entries since I began my writing journey more than a year ago. There are times when my process just requires witnessing the internal storm and waiting for inspiration.

A ten month period of accelerated growth has just completed. There was a gradual perception of contention developing within my caregiving team generated by one particular caregiver. A sense of avoiding conflict on my part accompanied by knowing that confronting the discord would not be simple caused the conflict to spread.

Objectively, the caregiver in question is a good person but has limited interpersonal skills, and when the hostility began to be directed at me personally I knew that inaction was not acceptable. I could not afford to have unresolved conflict in my 'field' and expect to maintain an environment of healing.

When the hostility began to escalate, I used these circumstances as a mode of practicing nonviolent communication. Initially this was very empowering and effective, however as the aberrant behavior escalated it became clear to me that I needed to be more assertive. I needed to show up in a powerful way without adding to the aggression.

I meditated on this and it became clear to me that I had to meet the aggression head on. I recognized that this was part of my 'soul teaching'...*of owning my power.* At a point in my journey where I have minimal physical strength, cowering from intimidation is the last thing I need.

I began to see this challenge as an opportunity for which I was grateful. My *'teacher'* was formidable and I could concurrently feel love and appreciation for her. The metaphor that came to me in a vision was that of a samurai warrior. I needed to meet each aggressive thrust with equal power.

Proof of my effectiveness would be evident if the aggression either escalated or was neutralized. My weapon was fierce honesty without wavering. I could not have carried this off successfully without being grounded in empathy for Self and 'other'. My nonviolent communication group questioned my intention initially, but my clarity was unshakable...*and the results were without question.*

Despite the significance of my progress, and perhaps as a result of this shift, profound anxiety was still present. Due to the changes that were consciously set in motion, there was no primary caregiver living on my property for many weeks. The level of anxiety I experienced was irrational when I considered how independent I was 90% of the time. Logic did not diminish the anxiety, however, and as a result I began to interview people from a place of desperation and fear.

When I saw this pattern clearly, I chose to forgo my present strategy. It came to me that I needed to take a month and clear the energy on my property for the first time in four years. No decisions were to be made during that time. Despite the overwhelming anxiety, I felt confident that this was the right decision. A batik style painting adorns my wall which reads, *"Let Go and Let God."* This message constantly challenged me during this pivotal month.

As the month progressed, I was able to put energy into the studio building where the new primary caregiver would live. I completely repaired and repainted the walls and had a shamanic healer clear the energy of both buildings. Not surprisingly, she found that the energy was inextricably entwined in a synergistic way between the buildings.

After a month, my anxiety continued but my relationship to it shifted. After many interviews I found myself with three viable options for primary caregivers, although none were without at least one complication. Unexpectedly, a caregiver with whom I'd had a fortuitous history came to me and requested the relationship. We had visited this possibility in the past, but the timing was never right.

Once again I am grateful for the teachings that occur when I have faith and do the right thing. Letting go of my familiar fears and trusting a deeper...*'Knowing'* liberates both myself and others. This may not have been my last encounter with *standing my ground* but each time I am able to move from victimization to empowerment *I am reaching a critical mass toward that end.*

MY GREEN LIGHT IS ON OR THE TAO OF KENNY-REVISITED

Blog Entry: **September 15, 2013**

"It is because you believe that you are born that you fear death. Who is it that was born? Who is it that dies? Look within. What was your face before you were born? Who you are, in reality, was never born and never dies. Let go of who you think you are and become who you have always been." – Steven Levine

My Skype slogan reads, *"If my green light is on, I am still in my body."* This statement may sound shallow and maybe even offensive but it also expresses my acceptance of the limitlessness of the Spirit - a concept I have learned while living with a chronic, life-threatening illness.

I've had a harrowing few weeks, the dreaded influenza bacteria was inadvertently brought into my space by a loving caregiver. I call her the...*'sacred initiator'* because she was a carrier who had sensitively offered to not work that fateful Monday but I rejected her offer after having been given the choice. After all, many of my caregivers have had children in the past who became ill and I was unaffected, *Why would this time be any different?*

Thirteen hours after contact, I developed a sore throat and swollen glands. It had been years since I'd had a respiratory infection. The first symptom I experienced was profound weakness on the stationary bike. I was weaker than I had ever been, including my first few times on the bicycle eight months prior.

With much optimism, I journeyed forward with the feeling that this was another initiation of sorts. It was an opportunity to engage in a certain curiosity and not fall prey to fear. This was particularly challenging, however, since the infectious disease specialists I met with eighteen months ago told me that if I contracted pneumonia, there would be only one antibiotic I had not developed a resistance to.

Three days after the weakness on the bicycle, the trajectory was apparent. It became clear to Matney and me that my breathing had entered a danger zone...*we needed to call 911.*! If you know me well, it takes a lot for me to surrender my autonomy and asked for professional help. Matney wondered if she should have called earlier, but she was reminded, *"do you think you would have convinced Aliyah before she was ready?!"* Enough said! The teaching of 'listening to the authority within' is, I believe, one of my central lifetime teachings.

As it turned out, the ambulance ride was the most fun part of this latest adventure! Once we made the decision to call 911, I had the sense that *"help was on the way,"* and I didn't have to do it all alone. The EMTs were well known to me by reputation and we spoke of horse riding and writing all the way to Heart of the Rockies Medical Center in Salida. During triage in the emergency room, Mike and Randy were particularly helpful.

The chest x-ray revealed pleural effusion most likely caused by this virulent infection. IV antibiotics were started immediately and, contrary to the infectious disease doctor's prediction, within twenty-four hours the infection was neutralized, the diagnosis of pneumonia was affirmed with the symptom of congestion being the worst of the experience. After only three days I was discharged. This might've been a little early, but ultimately I was able to resume my protocols and rehabilitative programs sooner. Never have I identified with Kenny's character from South Park more than I have this week!

One thing I've noticed about myself, after being rigorous with my protocols during the last two years, is that my healing capacity is tremendous. It isn't that I won't develop serious issues, but when I do they clear up quickly and unexpectedly to some.

About five months ago, I tore a ligament in the transverse arch of my foot. The physical therapist told me it would likely not heal, but I could get an artificial arch for it to hurt less. I immediately secured one on Amazon and three weeks later it was healed. There are many more examples, the latest being *pleural effusion caused by pneumonia*.

I frequently gaze up at the figurine of Kenny that Jordan gave me and identify with Kenny's resilience. Two weeks after the initial sore throat, I am resuming my rehabilitation. I don't mean to white wash my experience of the last two weeks as there have been a few times I wanted to jump out of my skin.

The support of my friends, children and caregivers has been immeasurable. Casey called me daily in the hospital, which was not an easy task given that someone had to come to my room to answer it for me. Due to her persistence, it happened. There was also an ongoing thread of my loved ones communicating through e-mail, for which I am grateful.

I'm sure that during the next few weeks my healing will be as tumultuous as has been my experience over the last ten years, but at this point I'm happy to report that...*my green light is still on!*

THE BODY AS MESSENGER

Blog Entry: September 21, 2013

"The world can seem marvelously convincing until death comes and evicts us from our hiding place." - Sogyal Rinpoche, a Tibetan master.

I find it interesting that when I am feeling confusion and despair I sometimes imagine that running to the medical establishment would provide the certainty that I am yearning for.

Years of ambiguous symptoms and a virtually untreatable illness however, has always made this behavior seem unfruitful.

There is often an almost unbearable crescendo of panic that builds during times of uncertainty. When I developed the courage to face the chaos head on and allow myself to feel the futility of the circumstances, whatever they might be at the time, I dropped finally into a state of deep listening. There is a certain peace that comes from turning *toward* the conflict, which reassures me that...*I am on the right track.* It can be very limiting to view the body as a cold isolated entity, but much can be learned from observing somatic processes with empathy and curiosity.

One of my caregivers described an interesting practice her father initiated within her family. When one of the children in her family became ill, the family member demonstrating symptoms was placed in the center of a circle and urged to discern and describe why they were ill. It was unacceptable for the individual to minimize the explanation by saying that they, for example, came in contact with bacteria or a virus - since we are always surrounded by bacteria. The family member was required to describe a scenario that led to the breakdown of the body, which often involved eating too much sugar, telling a lie or having a fight with a sibling. This practice taught the children about having integrity for one's actions and the power of...*the body-mind connection.*

What an education this form of inquiry can provide! To understand that illnesses don't just happen to the body in isolation, but that certain circumstances must be in place for illness to happen. It is important to realize that often the illness is a process that brings the body into balance. It is not the enemy where war needs to be waged. It is also important to know that whatever one's physical state, the body is desperately trying to heal itself or to come into balance. Often the body is misunderstood and is perceived to be betraying oneself, *Empathy is the most significant ingredient for healing to occur.*

That being said, there has been much turmoil during the last few months, culminating in my 60th birthday celebration. I had to face accelerating the conflict with my primary caregiver and the ultimate parting of our ways. I had to accommodate a succession of visitors during the summer, hire and train new caregivers and deal with the feelings invoked by reaching a 'milestone birthday' - one which I thought I might never reach. These circumstances engendered much joy as well, but my seeming inability to listen to my deeper internal feelings contributed to an emotional overload.

Perhaps all of this activity set the scene for the pneumonia to occur in August, after my immune system had become compromised by the cumulative level of stress. Since these issues involved my lungs, I thought to explore whether grief was triggered - in Chinese medicine the lungs represent areas where grief can collect.

Just prior to contact with the bacteria, I had an interaction with my former husband that was greatly disappointing. Grief was elicited by the interaction, both in the form of disappointment from the outcome as well as triggering mourning of my former life on the horse farm. Since I did not actively grieve at the moment, I needed to listen for the feelings that I'd buried and not released.

If we practice listening to the subtleties in our bodies, we can become astute students. If we miss the innuendos they will likely morph into symptoms to get our attention. I acknowledge with some regret that I have often needed *'the sledgehammer approach!'* Knowing this, I have made it my 'Sacred practice' to become even more sensitive. We can learn to *'hear our bodies'* and perhaps, with Grace, begin to practice *'the feather approach.'*

ONE PREREQUISITE FOR A CALL TO SERVICE

Blog Entry: December 16, 2013

"Limit gives form to the limitless." – Pythagoras

Is it considered consensual if I was curious and only nine years old at the time? What about if he was only a teenager himself? Although these questions are rhetorical and have been adequately answered long ago, nothing is black and white when it comes to emotions.

On the scope of *sexual abuse*, what happened to me was more benign, which made it all the more confusing to come to terms with. As is the case with many of these situations, there was coercion *but no violence*. I suspect that it ended in a good way with me saying "*no more*". All in all, it was an empowering outcome. I never realized that before writing this. It is interesting how these experiences can shape one's personality.

Over time, I treated this in the same way I treated other traumatic experiences in my life. I talked about it in therapy, I utilized role-playing techniques, and worked in many spiritual contexts to get to the other side of the feelings. Just as I felt ready to talk to the '*perpetrator*', he came to me to apologize. It was once suggested to me by a spiritual healer that this experience happened to heal an unresolved karmic issue. There are many aspects of this childhood trauma that brought unexpected and synergistic healing for all concerned.

It has been said that many therapists choose the profession of psychotherapy because they need healing themselves. The archetype of *the wounded healer* describes a person who heals from the wound sustained by being in a human body and having traumatic experiences with other people. I believe that we incarnate to evolve emotionally and to ascend spiritually.

Healing from childhood trauma is a necessary prerequisite for providing psychotherapy to others. During Werner Erhart's training in California in the 80s, I received the culminating piece to heal this issue. Unless a return to empathy for all parties involved has happened, the issue is not complete. I realize that empathy and forgiveness happen naturally if the feelings have been allowed to be felt fully and completely.

When observing the candlelight ceremony honoring the one year anniversary of the tragedy in Newtown, CT, a mother of one of the slain children acknowledged that two more candles needed to be added to the existing twenty-six. After all, the perpetrator had taken his own life and the life of his mother prior to the slaughter in the elementary school. No one had considered the devastation of mental illness that ravaged this young perpetrator and which held the mother hostage for many years. By including these two souls, in my opinion, the picture is complete...*for the greatest healing to occur.*

After I returned from California I started my nearly ten year stretch at the community mental health center working as a psychotherapist. I learned to recognize the relationship between my healing and my call to service. I knew there are no accidents, that I was where I needed to be and that I was living the experiences necessary for my healing and that of others. During the 1990s I wrote a poem that helped to validate and integrate this issue in my life:

THE SUBSTANCE

Sticky, viscous liquid

Alive with movement and intention Like soldiers marching to battle.

The pungent smell of arousal Awakens my senses As it warms my heart

And speaks to my need.

But when did the soldiers declare mutiny Turning against the host?

When does the salvation become the destroyer?

And finally the climax, the ultimate betrayal With a slash through the heart so deep There's no hope for repair.

All is lost

In a desolate landscape. And inward, a broken heart.

In the dark she cries

For the fragments of her spirit Silently praying for the spark To ignite her soul.

ROOTS OF LOVE THROUGH GENERATIONS

Blog Entry: January 7, 2014

"Once the realization is accepted that even between the closest human beings infinite distances continue, a wonderful living side by side can grow." - Rainer Maria Rilke

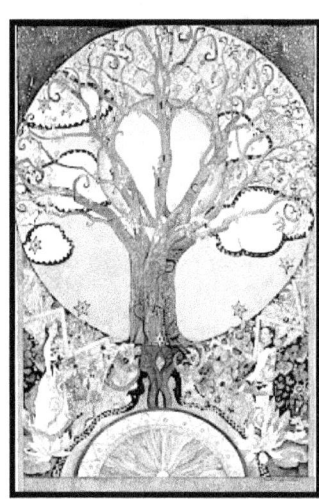

As I grew up in Pennsylvania, I felt disconnected and alienated from my family. My mother contracted a mysterious illness for ten of my formative years while my father worked excessively in his high-end furniture business. Around the dinner table if you didn't discuss the furniture business...*you were invisible.*

I learned to use both humor and negative behavior to be seen.

My paternal grandfather was known to be more of a humanitarian than a businessman and leaned politically toward socialism. My father attended a socialist school during his high school years. This school was comprised of working class Jewish emigrants from Eastern Europe and focused on social injustice. Perhaps it was watching his mother refuse food during the Great Depression so that her children were able to eat that influenced my father to shift toward capitalism.

My father began working when he was in high school and transformed his father's used furniture store into a high-end business. As I watched my father's obsessive behavior over the years, I developed a love-hate relationship with capitalism and decided that I would never make a choice to work in businesses to sustain a materialistic life style - not after witnessing my father's hyper-focus on business and the resulting neglect of his family.

From an early age I was drawn to a life of service. I visited people in the hospital in my neighborhood and worked in summer camps for developmentally disabled children. I had little interest in capitalism, instead I became idealistic and wanted...*to heal the world*.

However, in addition to my antipathy toward capitalism, I had an abject fear of not being able to support myself. Building confidence in their children had not been a primary focus for my parents, they were much more focused on survival. They were both first generation American born and carried much trauma from their respective histories. Achievement orientation was not a central part of my upbringing.

My first serious boyfriend however, helped to instill this quality in me during my college years and I became the president of the freshman women's honor society and later vice president of the psychological honor society. I graduated cum laude from the University of Miami and received my Masters from Tulane University as an A student.

When I moved from Miami to New Orleans for graduate school, I finally felt like I belonged somewhere and it would be in New Orleans where I would truly grow up. It was in New Orleans where I found a succession of teachers to help me heal many of my wounds from childhood and where I would face my fear of not being able to support myself financially, but it would take a surprising and circuitous path.

I wanted to know how to *serve*. I entered a premed program and was invited to join the premed honor society. When I realized that I would have to redo my whole undergraduate degree however, which was comprised primarily of social sciences, I decided that practicing psychotherapy could provide all the service I would need to feel fulfilled in a career.

Soon after this decision was made, I met, fell in love with and married my second husband. A year later, my son was born and we moved to the northshore where I volunteered at my daughter's school and participated in her extracurricular activities. Needing to contribute to the family income, I secured a job at a furniture store in New Orleans run by a Jewish family. I know, *the irony eluded me at the time*!

When I began working at the furniture store I took to it like a fish to water. I sold three times that of the other salespeople and was offered a sales management position. To me selling furniture was a gas, it was effortless. What I found most satisfying, however, was the unconscious tendency I had toward working therapeutically with my customers.

When working with couples, I found a way to empower the disempowered member of the dyad. This method proved strangely effective in influencing the outcome and ultimate satisfaction gleaned from the sale. On one occasion, a woman disclosed that her daughter was raising her mentally disabled grandchild. She described a particularly challenging scenario that her daughter was managing. I can remember saying to this grandmother, *"God knows who to give these children to."* The next time the woman came in to see me she reported that she had been deeply moved by our interaction - she'd had a mini breakdown and had secured a therapist.

I was beginning to feel that selling furniture was feeding an addictive part of me even though I could, in fact, support myself. It was becoming clear that in order to return to practicing psychotherapy I had to take myself much more seriously. I had to find the confidence internally that had not been forthcoming. I recognized the significance of returning to my roots through the business I had adamantly and righteously rejected...*I had come full circle.*

The success and satisfaction that I found was a complete surprise. By completing the circle from resentment to humility I was able to have gratitude for the sacrifices my father and grandfather had made so that our family's physical survival was secured. Now I had the freedom to choose how I would express that life.

It was from the sacrifices of my ancestors that I had the freedom to choose a life of service and social action. I wonder if my grandfather would be surprised to know how much he indirectly influenced my life. He was known as a quiet man, one who would cross the street to avoid a customer who owed him money so as to not embarrass the customer.

I never knew my grandfather as I was the youngest of my siblings and he had contracted a degenerative neurological disease in his later years. Ultimately, it is ironic that I probably had more in common with this man whom I'd never known than my mother and father.

Now that I am in my later years, living with this degenerative neurological illness and being so far away from my grandchildren, I can hope that there is an unseen way that love and its influence manifests...*Perhaps this is yet another unexpected teaching from my grandfather.*

DON'T JUST DO SOMETHING, SIT THERE

Blog Entry: Febuary 17, 2014

"If you want to awaken all of humanity, then awaken all of yourself. If you want to eliminate all of the suffering in the world, then eliminate all that is dark and negative in yourself. Truly, the greatest gift you have to give is that of your own self transformation." - Lao Tze

My life is a sitting meditation. That is what I do twenty-three hours a day, I sit. If a disturbing thought arises I cannot distract myself. I cannot stand up and leave the room or take a hike on the trail. I am a captive audience. When I ponder who my captor might be, the answer is unequivocally...*my higher self.*

My *Self* is a benevolent captor that has unexpectedly become a liberator. Sitting by myself hour after hour, day after day, month after month, and year after year, I've become more comfortable than I've ever been with myself. It is interesting to consider what has led to this liberation.

Some of my greatest obstacles to knowing who I truly am have been erroneous beliefs. The greatest such belief was that I am *alone in this large universe,* which triggered my greatest fear, *the fear of being helpless.* Being unable to walk or feed myself renders me totally helpless in a literal sense. Yet I have never felt as powerful as I do now. I have never felt as connected to something greater than myself, both internally and externally until this point in my life and becoming liberated from my greatest fear is both humbling and heartening.

Another obstacle toward self-actualization involved having a strong, reliable, and attractive body. This was both a gift and a hindrance as it often distracted me from connecting with my inner being, which, in turn, has led to liberating my spirit. My physical strength was a gift when I needed to create my earlier life including my home and career and raising my children. However, once they were raised I seemed to be treading in the waters of my fears, desperately trying to prove to myself that I was not alone and helpless. Being in serial relationships never seemed to affirm a connectedness that was mirrored internally. Having been successful at athletic competitions never seemed to inoculate me from feeling a sense of helplessness.

What I have noticed while sitting in meditation most days is that my mind and spirit have deepened exponentially. This process has inadvertently created distance between myself and many who were once close to me. There has been much to mourn in my life, yet there has been much to celebrate as well. I can even celebrate my ability to mourn, it takes courage and determination to mourn and move on.

There have been many times when I've moved through this process kicking and screaming. There've been times when I resisted and avoided the inevitable. I believe that is part of why we are in human bodies.

Being still, day after day, has allowed me to enter a state of liminality, where dissolution of a previous order can happen. Liminality (from the Latin word limen: a threshold) yields much uncertainty and fluidity while processing through emotional states. Entering the liminal state has provided an accelerated course in life.

Although it is not necessary for most people to enter into such an intense initiation to progress spiritually, on a conscious level I felt like I had no choice. In this body, with this personality, the time was now. It was time to take...*the Leap*. Here is a poem that I wrote in 1989, just *prior* to the first symptom:

TAKE THE LEAP

The power is running through me now. The brakes in energy are excruciating. Synapses suck. As it jumps does it increase in power? The movement just before the jump surge is an eternity—the place where agony lives, where death becomes a real possibility.

Life is in the jump. (The vocalized sigh gives life. Expansion for creation. The echoes of the sigh bring community. Love. Breath.)

It jumps because it has to. It Knows no other Way. There is no consideration of consequences. No sureness that land lies beyond the trajectory.

We grow. We make our choices. "it" doesn't care what our choices are. We create our experiences. "It" continually provides us the opportunity to be in the Love.

It doesn't matter what one chooses. One must choose and move on.

Take the Leap

CHAPTER EIGHT
THE CANARY IN THE COAL MINE

"At last, having conquered the demons without and within, the hero has earned the right to live life as he chooses…" Joseph Campbell

LIFE IN THE HOLY

Blog Entry: **March 30, 2014**

"And the day came when the risk to remain tight in a bud was more painful that the risk it took to blossom." - Anais Nin

A decade ago, the trajectory of this illness was looking like a steep dive into certain and impending doom. I prepared my children and myself for the worst. When I returned to Pennsylvania, it had become clear that the resources available for my psychological and spiritual sustenance were anemic. I didn't know how I was going to do it, but at a certain point I knew I had to return to my home in Crestone, Colorado. Crestone is where I chose to move after Katrina. It is a magical town where most of the world's spiritual centers are represented, a place where I could heal my heart, my heart that was shattered after the diagnosis and the hurricane. David and I packed what we did not sell and moved to Colorado.

I'd surrendered to the use of a wheelchair prior to the journey to Colorado. During the move I had the horrific accident shattering my right femur somewhere in Missouri and my femur was surgically reconstructed in Lincoln, Nebraska. The accident left no ambiguity about my physical limitations. I was unable to bear weight for many months. This rendered me virtually helpless and the incident revealed a major fault line in my marriage.

When David asked for a divorce, I was not prepared for a future with this number of...*unknowns*. I was terrified of what my future might bring. Fortunately, I had close friends and family to rely on for emotional support, *and rely on them I did.*

Now I can look back in amazement at the level of *letting go* I needed to accomplish to be in this present *'place of acceptance'*. My life today in no way resembles my life just six short years ago. I can understand why few marriages survive this rigorous curriculum and as I surrender more completely, my life appears monastic...*Holy.*

During times of surrender my mission becomes clear and joyful. The humanitarian life I have chosen, *or has chosen me*, has become more subtle and almost...*mysterious* as I transition to a deeper understanding. During the times I refuse to accept my rigorous assignment however, I fall into dense grief regarding the past.

This dynamic provides a vital lesson for *living in the present moment* and I clearly understand the expression, *"all we have is now."* As I let go of my secular life, the level of *connection* that is available to me with myself and others deepens considerably and I can let go of the belief that...*life with a functional body is central and necessary.*

I can understand and accept why others might have a hard time subscribing to such a rigorous journey. It is understandable that the divorce rate is so high when a life-threatening, degenerative illness is introduced. Back then, if I had been able to imagine the joy that was possible, *instead of wanting to be rescued from hopelessness* I might have presented a more positive outlook regarding the future.

Perhaps, to be fully experienced and integrated such a rigorous and profound journey needed to be a solitary one. I believe that everything happens in the right order and at the right time. As I surrender to a greater *Story of Holiness*, the sense of mundane loneliness disappears. I am able to connect to the unseen world...*heaven on earth*, where love and connectedness are a given and where everything is possible and happening simultaneously. This is a place that is always available to me, to us...*if we open to the Holy.*

AN OPTIMISTIC RETROSPECTIVE

Blog Entry: **April 29, 2014**

"As I walked out the door toward the gate that would lead to my freedom, I knew if I didn't leave my bitterness and hatred behind, I would still be in prison." - Nelson Mandela

I come from a family of survivors. Having been second-generation American-born on both sides of my family, I have felt the effects of religious and political persecution on a psychological and almost a *genetic* level.

The trauma gets filtered down through enculturation. Children experience their parent's trauma through a process not unlike osmosis.

Having been an immigrant and an orphan, my paternal grandmother was a domestic worker when she came to my home town of Scranton, Pennsylvania as a young adult. Knowing that my grandfather was single, her family offered him $500 to marry her. Regardless of the unconventional beginning, they had a strong marriage that lasted nearly sixty years.

As soon as he was old enough my father went to work at my grandfather's used furniture store to help support his family...*he was on a mission.* I can honestly say that *because of my father's support,* I never went hungry nor wanted for anything material.

My father would have saved every nickel he made if it weren't for my mother. She taught him to relax and spend his money. One quality my mother possessed was unequivocal generosity. Not only did she teach my father to enjoy the fruits of his hard work, but she was also a well-known philanthropist in the community.

From an early age I felt uncomfortable with the level of financial abundance in my family. Perhaps my oversensitivity to the struggles of others stimulated this response. The disparity of peoples' living situations affected me deeply as a young child.

Ironically, I resented my parent's wealth because my emotional needs were sacrificed by my father's 'mission', which would later be called workaholism. As much material abundance there was in my family, there was an equal amount of emotional deprivation. Perhaps the generations of struggle in Eastern Europe had a cumulative effect that would take generations to clear. The way I have come to look at it, the task of my parent's generation was to assure physical survival and it was my generation's task and privilege to improve that quality of life by finding ways to meet our emotional needs.

As I matured, I've developed more appreciation for the financial stability afforded by my father's hard work. Being the youngest of my siblings carried with it a sense of dependency and inadequacy common to most 'babies of the family.' After acquiring a Masters degree in a field which I felt great passion, I was faced with not just a fear of survival but a virtual certainty of failure. Once I secured a job in my field however, I began to feel more adequate. As I began to excel the previous inadequacies slowly faded. Over time I began to feel more independent as my financial solvency became more reliable.

After passing my state licensure exam and beginning a private practice, I visited a new challenge. I needed to charge clients what I believed my work was worth. This created a new challenge, that of evaluating my own self-worth! As my self-esteem increased, the people with whom I associated reflected that quality. We do attract what we believe internally about ourselves.

I was carrying the mantle to begin meeting the emotional needs of our generation. We survived generations of pogroms in Russia and concentration camps in Eastern Europe. Children of our generation have carried the *'gifts and the curses'* of the unresolved issues of the previous generations. We survived immobilizing feelings of inadequacy, physical illnesses and potentially debilitating addictions.

I believe present and future generations will carry less and less of the trauma as they are imbued with greater skills to meet the challenges they face. Seeing my children and my grandchildren, I have much hope for our future.

As I said previously, I come from a family of survivors. My family has been privileged, because of those who came before us, to be able to do our share to heal our collective humanity.

GETTING THROWN, SOMETIMES

Blog Entry: June 2, 2014

"First I was raw; then I was cooked; now I am burnt." - *Rumi*

Okay, sometimes I get totally thrown! During those times, there is no escape from my mind, from the feeling in my chest. It vacillates between a Shakespearean play and a banal soap opera.

I have some control for redirection but the intensity remains unaffected...*I sit.*

I love where I sit. Right now I'm facing snowcapped fourteen thousand foot mountains, or 'fourteeners' to the locals. I would rather be here than anywhere else. I sit and examine my life. It is a sacred task and one for which I feel much gratitude.

Who gets to do this? When something from my past feels incomplete, it gets tweaked. If there is something that I haven't said to someone, I see it and say it. There is a flow with every relationship in my life. I have corrected the imbalance of giving too much...*I have learned to receive.*

I believe that when we leave this majestic world, like most near-death experiences portray, we have a 'life review.' I'm fortunate to begin that self-reflection while still in my body. There is an old Hasidic saying, *"on your deathbed, you never say, I should have worked more."* Whether this chair in which

I sit is a deathbed or a temporary place of rest *is merely a matter of semantics.*

I have partial use of one hand, that's it. From a competitive swimmer, runner, and horse rider, this is my…*'Sacred Curriculum.'* I accept this curriculum and all that it involves. Would I rather be riding my horse or snow skiing? Honestly, there are moments I would. Would I rather be flying to New York City to be with my children and grandchildren? Clearly, there are moments, many moments, that I would. However, doing this *Work* is what I am here to do in the present moment. All I have, all we all have…*is the present moment.*

It is in the present moment where true joy lives. For me, the past brings grief and the future…*fear.* That is generally true for everyone, whether dealing with a life-threatening illness or not. The present moment is where I try to live. Our bodies join with our spirits to partner with us in this endeavor.

Everybody gets thrown sometimes, It is a sacred practice to metaphorically pick ourselves up, brush ourselves off, and begin again! It is the *'means* to the end' that grows our soul. It is that perseverance that grows self-love…*I believe that this is the essence of why we are here.*

EXPERIMENTAL PSYCHOLOGY REVISITED: HEALING THE SACRED FEMININE-PART 1

Blog Entry: **June 22, 2014**

"Between stimulus and response, there is a space. In that space lies our freedom and power to choose our response. In our response lies our growth and freedom." - Viktor Frankl

I have an hypothesis.

Some individuals with a progressive form of multiple sclerosis become regressed physically to a primal or even infantile state of development in order to heal our deepest wound from this lifetime - that is, an interruption in the bonding process with the primary, maternal parental figure. Early in this disease process, I had the insight that I might become completely disabled to heal this fracture.

This insight came in a flash and I did not have the courage to entertain the concept in much depth at the time *due to my paralyzing fear.* Coincidentally, around the same time I had contact with another woman facing similar circumstances. She referred to her mother as a 'mommy dearest' type. I thought it was coincidental that my mother, too, was certainly not wired for nurturance and could be quite combative and emotionally abusive during her worst moments.

My mother was raised with male siblings exclusively and she was strongly bonded to her father as opposed to her mother. This family constellation mirrored mine exactly.

For at least two generations there was little feminine bonding. Although I had many girlfriends in my childhood, I identified as a tomboy. When I entered intensive psychotherapy during my twenties, the therapists suggested that I associate with women. My greatest therapeutic intervention involved a triangle with a male and a female, I was convinced that I was being rejected by the male and while doing the emotional work and feeling much vulnerability a deeper pattern revealed itself.

To my shock, it was the fear of the loss of my female friend that devastated me! Light was shed on this illusory pattern in my life. Understanding that my emotional needs with my mother would not be met, I transferred these needs to my father. This revealed a recurring pattern of making men overly important in my life...*and now I knew why.*

After this revelation, my life turned completely around. I became much more available for deeply fulfilling relationships with women. I still had a long way to go in healing *'the Feminine'* but at least I was finally on the right track. My relationships with men were still mostly compulsive, but something significant was balancing internally.

In 1990, during the beginning stages of subtle neurological symptoms, I met a woman who would be my mentor for the next fifteen years and began Holotropic breathwork - an experiential form of transpersonal psychology that opened my world to the deepest healing of my life. Mathilde was unconventional to say the least, but for the first time I was able to let in nurturing by a woman!

Mathilde observed that my process of letting in nurturance was like feeding a Biafran baby, sometimes one drop at a time. I traveled to New Mexico many times a year to do this Sacred work and reveled in the freedom that this unconventional modality provided. There were many nights that I climbed into Mathilde's waterbed and slept beside her. Never had I felt this comfortable with a woman.

Finally, I was able to see my pattern of entering into serial, addictive relationships with men. I was able to extricate myself from this pattern to spend three years developing a relationship with myself exclusively. Initially I felt terror at the prospect, but over time I found tremendous joy as I deepened my understanding of who I was. As I grew, my profession grew and I had the feeling that my clients' experiences deepened as well. It was soon after that that I met David.

EXPERIMENTAL PSYCHOLOGY, REVISITED: HEALING THE SACRED FEMININE-PART 2

Blog Entry: June 26, 2014

"This is to love: to fly toward a secret sky, to cause a hundred veils to fall each moment." - Rumi

I had originally met David many years earlier at a Gurdjieff school in which I briefly participated. Later we met again when he brought an 'at risk' adolescent for treatment at the mental health clinic where I was employed. I remember that we shared a mission to keep this child alive, with the hope that she would eventually thrive. Still later, we reconnected at a play in Abita Springs and I felt both a connection and an aversion, which confused me.

Around this time I was preparing for another personal retreat in New Mexico to do breathwork. I'd completed the fundamental healing with *'mother'*, had become comfortable with my internal feminine and, as always, I was open to whatever next piece my healing would reveal.

During my breathwork session I had a vision. I was transported to Egypt for a sacred healing process. I was lying on a table. The 'healer' was a cat which walked around my body and spread healing energy. This scene was like an initiation ritual which allowed me to deepen my spiritual process. After the session, I created artwork and remained contemplative.

The following day I had an astrology reading with a local practitioner. The session reaffirmed the trajectory of my healing process. I felt a strong connection with the astrologer, in fact the session ran longer than most of her sessions.

After returning to Arroyo Seco, thoughts of the astrologer stayed in my mind. I decided to ask her to join me for tea and I brought her flowers. I didn't completely understand what was happening to me internally, but I felt giddy and somewhat undone. While reflecting on my visit and my breathwork session, it occurred to me that the astrologer's name was Kat. Was there some significance to *'being initiated by a cat?.'*

I was filled with a mixture of curiosity, excitement, and terror. I considered what a decision like this would have on my life. I impulsively called David long-distance, which injected energy into that relationship. I realized that I knew that I was entering this relationship with David out of fear, but I could feel comfort that it was at least *conventional*. I remember telling David about this encounter and I shared my suspicion that an encounter with Kat would bring deep healing on the feminine level. He empathized, but he personally preferred for it not to become actualized.

As it was, I stayed with David. It is likely that the illness that was in remission would have exacerbated either way. I can't know the answer from this vantage point, but the illness, in fact, progressed!

Two decades later, I have few regrets for the decisions I have made. As I sit in my solitary meditative space and look with awe at the profound healing in my life, I'm remembering my hypothesis, that this illness can be an opportunity to heal the deepest wound for a woman - *disconnection from the Feminine.* While watching a documentary regarding Edie Windsor and her revolutionary fight for marriage equality, I learned that her partner had lived with a progressive form of multiple sclerosis until 2008, when she succumbed to the illness. When I watched Thea, I was struck by how unusual it was to see another woman so profoundly disabled, yet as joyful as I am. I was curious about Thea's early mothering and it was revealed that her mother had died when she was an infant...*coincidence?*

I am not at all concluding that one's sexual preference leads to deeper healing. I also believe that masculine/feminine energy is not necessarily gender-based, however in my situation, my healing had to come through women. I can see a deep level of healing that has occurred through the love and care of my female caregivers. I have developed an ease with them and with my body that I never could have imagined possible. There was a level of self-hatred that I lived with on the level of the body that is no longer there. It is less important to me how the self-hatred gets cleared, but that it gets replaced with volumes of self-love.

Thank you for entering into this Journey with me and witnessing the ups and downs, the losses and wins of an ordinary soul having...*an extraordinary human existence.*

Your love comes to me in a gentle, elemental way
As with a breath it fills me nurturing every cell
Like with the rocking of a chair
my comfort and sureness deepen

With each wane like the gentle stroking from Mother
To brush away the tears
And the sound of a love song that echoes through the years

Shows me a place to go
Where Her ample lap so safe, so sweet
Gently rocks me to sleep

SHUT-IN, BEDRIDDEN, HOUSEBOUND... OH MY!

Blog Entry: July 2, 2014

"Freedom's just another word for nothing else to lose."–Janis Joplin

Shut-in, Bedridden, Housebound. It doesn't matter what you call it, personally, these adjectives make my skin crawl. Somebody referred to me the other day as bedridden. She meant well, but I felt like I had been punched in the solar plexus.

Are those terms a physical description or a state of mind? Are they legal terms or something that determines one's disability status? All I know is that neither I nor any of my friends relate those terms to me.

I sit in my comfortable reclining chair twenty-two hours a day, seven days a week. Every few months I leave the house to go to an appointment. Does this relieve me of the description of being housebound? The use of these terms reduces my vitality. If someone didn't know me personally, these adjectives might elicit pity or perhaps fear, which is always underneath pity in my opinion. No one who knows me would ever consider describing me with any of those terms.

Last Christmas I had a traumatic experience that made this whole discussion personal. I received a request on Facebook to have a visit from a group of carolers from Crestone. Christmas carols have been a part of my history despite being raised Jewish. After all, for nearly six years during my time in New Orleans, I was an active participant in an interracial, interfaith, gospel choir! During Christmas we frequently sang at the St. Louis Cathedral in the French Quarter. Singing music during the holidays was familiar to me for connecting with the holiday spirit. At least that is what I thought would happen when I agreed to the request.

An hour after the carolers were scheduled to arrive and just before my next appointment, they made their appearance. It has been said that Crestone is made up of meditators, mystics, and misfits and I am sure that I could have received all three labels by different people at different times in my life. As thirty people straggled in, an hour late, my enthusiasm began to wane abruptly. On one level, I knew they were well-meaning, but the setup was disturbing. I should have been alerted to this possibility when the organizer mentioned, *"we are a group of people who go caroling to the housebound."* I didn't catch it at the moment, but later I noticed myself wondering *who was the housebound person we were going to sing to?*

They filed into my round living room en masse and began singing the common, ordinary Christmas songs my choir never sang, *I began to feel the depth of my disillusionment.* As I looked around, the energy in the room felt *"charitable",* to put it kindly. I could feel that the singers felt that they were singing to the *"poor, disabled shut-in."* I started to compulsively make jokes to at least let them know that I was clever and that my mind was clear. The message I desperately wanted to convey was, *"it's okay! Really, I'm okay! It isn't as dire as you think! It's all going to be okay! This is just a temporary costume!"* I felt sorry for them, they looked so pained.

When they finally left I felt diminished, marginalized maybe even *objectified*. It took a few hours to clear the energy of their collective projections. I shudder when I remember those feelings and I know that it is essential that the people I surround myself with be responsible for their own projections and that they know who I am and that this illness is...*not me*. The visitors that Christmas day thought they were in their role of being *charitable and magnanimous*. They only saw my body. They were not seeing me, the brave soul undertaking this courageous curriculum and working through my deepest challenge of powerlessness to increase my love of Self.

I learned that day that I am more vulnerable to other people's unconscious projections than I realized. I learned that the terms shut-in, housebound, and bedridden are merely states of mind and they can be dangerously reductive. I learned that one needs to be responsible for one's own projections, *the feelings beneath their benevolence.* Many are not capable of this level of awareness so I need to be more vigilant, more protective of my vulnerability. I learned a lot that Christmas day.

I'm fortunate to say that everybody in my life on a daily basis sees *me*, beyond my costume for this particular role. I will use this as a teaching moment. Some of the most evolved souls enter the human body of seemingly vulnerable individuals: the homeless, alcoholics, and the mentally and/or physically disabled in order to grow and especially to serve humanity. When I was a small child, a religious woman who was close to me once told me that Karen, a mentally disabled child in the neighborhood, was an angel from God and that Karen would report back to God and let him know how she was being treated. Of course, there was the authoritative, punitive attitude placed on to a male God, but I received the message both on a literal level and a metaphysical level.

These descriptions can be superficial and innocent, but they have power. We need to be responsible for our projections which I believe are mostly fear-based, fear of the unknown or fear that *it* might happen to me or one of my loved ones.

Are we merely seeing the costume for this lifetime or are we seeing the Soul? If you would like to come to my home for a visit and are able to see me beyond the level of the body, you are very welcome. Come, share...*and be in the Holy with me.*

TRANSPARENCY: A GIFT OR A CURSE

Blog Entry: July 18, 2014

"Ring the bells that still can ring, forget your perfect offering. There is a crack, a crack in everything. That is how the light gets in." - Leonard Cohen

I have a different idea of transparency than most other people I know. I believe that we all have dirty laundry and it is only by airing it that we become clean.

I do not believe that anybody in a human body is devoid of dirt *or Shadow*, if we use the Jungian term. These disowned parts of ourselves are kept in a dark place through fear and self-hatred and it is in the healing of these painful emotions that transparency and authenticity emerge.

One of my caregivers once posed a question to me, beginning with, *"you don't have to answer this if it is too personal."* We both laughed hysterically because I am always so blatantly honest about everything and I responded, *"challenge me!" I* believe that being totally transparent is a virtue, although I understand that others might cringe and disagree.

When I look at what might be in the way of me sharing something deeply personal it seems to be some version of shame. Shame is a feeling that both causes suffering and reveals an area where healing is essential. I do not expect others to share in the level of transparency that I live, it just surprises me when I find so little consensus. Because of this, I began to look at what was the difference in my development.

In this endeavor, I've reflected on my life many years earlier while participating in intensive group psychotherapy. When conflict arose, it would be taken seriously as a block to intimacy and we would meet with one of the facilitators to remediate the tension. In each situation, I realized that the conflict was based on distortions of the truth between us. When the distortions were clarified, connection was restored. Because we trusted the group facilitators, the love between the group members grew exponentially. It was through this level of intimacy that I first began to believe in God. To me, God was not a punitive man spewing judgment from on high, he wasn't a bearded pilgrim in sandals, *It* was this feeling that began in my chest and radiated out to include everyone it touched.

It was in this community of beloved individuals that I saw that all anybody really wanted was to be loved, and once that was realized...*to be able to serve.* I came to see that conflict was merely confusion, either with one's self or another, or both. It was during that time that I realized that blockage to truth was merely misinformation. It became a sacred practice for me to dismantle my inner blocks to truth. To be able to speak my truth, unencumbered, was central to this practice. For me, the practice involved looking at the intention behind each statement I would make. I would ask myself what I was communicating and which of my needs it served, did it serve a higher need for integrity or did it meet a lower ego need? *Did the statement increase or decrease my vibration?*

As I began to work with groups, my working theory was realized on a deeper level. The dictum of confidentiality is the foundation for creating safety within groups of people. I believe, however, that at a certain point a dictum can become a hindrance to intimacy. I also believe that the degree of openness is dependent upon one's own personal development. Each person must decide for her or himself what they are comfortable with based on their own level of truth.

Until that point, I honor confidentiality implicitly yet I am clear that I do not require the same for myself. On the contrary, I believe that my internal work when shared with others, can have the power to effect change in them. That is where my passion lies, in pushing my boundaries toward transparency.

As I mentioned earlier, one has to achieve a certain level of development to have integrity and respect for self and others. One has to 'get right' with one's own 'shadow' for this level of consciousness to be integrated. Without coming to terms with one's own pain, collusion with other people's pain will likely occur.

Through all this I came to my central conclusion once again that as embodied humans our Work is to uncover our wounds, which will ultimately heal the pockets of self-hatred causing our suffering. It is through this sacred journey, while embodied...*that self-love can be realized.*

CAREGIVING-PART 2: A HOLOGRAPHIC PARADIGM

Blog Entry: July 24, 2014

"Each time we drop our masks and meet heart to heart... Each time we are able to remain open to suffering, despite our fear and defensiveness, we sense a love in us which becomes increasingly unconditional... Awakening from our sense of separateness is what we are called to do in all things."- Ram Dass

The practice of caregiving is changing as our culture ages and evolves. An old understanding of this practice involves a unilateral, unidirectional expression of support offered from the caregiver to the subject. However, as one develops more sophistication about the energetic exchanges between people, it becomes apparent that much more is happening during the interchange. From my experience, it is impossible for two people to interact intimately and not have complex and often unconscious forces operating on the dyad.

As the individuals become more sensitive to the subtleties of their interaction, the caregiver may begin to notice either an infusion or depletion of the respective energies. It is essential for the caregiver to explore these shifts in emotional and physical well-being if one is to become a more conscious care practitioner. It is only when these energetic shifts are perceived and acknowledged that the source of these effects can be understood. This is the process of self-reflection and Knowing Oneself. The better one knows one's self, the more satisfying relating to others will be and the more effective the caregiving relationship.

I believe that an individual's ability to render care effectively is directly related to his or her capacity for intimacy. This capacity is initially nurtured during infancy by the primary parental relationship. Although the parents are central to influencing the initial imprinting once the soul is incarnated, there will be many subsequent surrogates throughout one's life who will contribute to this capacity. I believe that developing one's capacity to love oneself and others is the work of most souls for the lifetime...*the karma is the dharma.*

My spiritual development involved both the physical body and the mind. Relatively early in life I chose the field of psychology as my life work, or what feels more accurate is psychology chose me. In my experience, many people choose psychology because it is they themselves who need healing and my situation was no different. As I have stated in previous blog entries, my relationship with my mother was complicated. Accordingly, every subsequent surrogate for healing this primal issue in my life reflected these complications, whether they were school teachers, coaches, therapists, husbands or in my later years, caregivers.

Although my mother clearly cared about me, my relationship with her was neither warm nor nurturing. The resulting vulnerability required psychological healing in order for wholeness to prevail. The subsequent surrogates provided a virtual tag team to assure future health and stability. A good deal of the unconscious material, the unresolved issues from childhood surfaced with my husbands, who provided much mirroring of my unexamined Shadow.

It is important to note that this mirroring process can be excruciating while the material remains unconscious. During my later years, caregivers would provide this mirroring in order for healing to occur. In such an intimate relationship, I cannot emphasize enough the need to become aware of unconscious dynamics...*to alleviate unnecessary suffering.*

During his last year, I have attracted a circle of caregivers including five women and two men. We meet every three weeks with Judith, a facilitator whose role is to mirror, reflect, and witness. She coined the phrase, *"care partnering"* and as integral parts of the system we all give and receive healing consciously.

Each individual is interested in his/her own healing and spiritual growth. It has become increasingly apparent to all the members of the circle that we have come together to consciously co-create a new paradigm for caregiving. The care circle is a moving, growing organism that feels more like a *hologram* than a collection of individuals. With the collective intention for increasing awareness of our archaic wounds, the healing manifests in the group as well as with each individual. There is a synergy that appears to be happening with this level of collective intention.

As baby boomers age, there will be more of a need for caregiving. It has been shown that keeping the elderly and/or disabled in their own homes is both economical and compassionate. It has been satisfying to witness how the level of *presence* engendered by each member of our circle has spread to other individuals in need of care in our community. I hope this can serve as a model for a new paradigm for offering care.

Arroyo Secco, New Mexico - 1999

OUR INTERRACIAL GOSPEL CHOIR

Blog Entry: **July 26, 2014**

"There are two ways of spreading light: to be the Candle or the Mirror that reflects it." - Edith Wharton

I previously wrote about my choir experiences, but I want to revisit this experience in a different way.

My two closest friends Mark and Diana introduced me to the choir. Mark was a tenor in the New Orleans Opera and Diana had been a musician most of her life.

I had taken voice lessons from an accomplished soprano who had sung at the St. Louis Cathedral in the French Quarter and piano lessons as a child, but I have never considered myself particularly gifted. Fortunately, when I began singing with the choir we did not have auditions.

Our African-American sisters and brothers had been singing in choirs since they were toddlers. For them, it was very much a part of their culture. For us Caucasians, it was our growing edge. We had to loosen our rigidity, which was both joyful and challenging for many. When Mark began singing solos, he was a courageous teacher for us to 'let go'. Initially, Mark was stiff, Diana's nickname for him was, *"white bread."* The humor in our choir helped tremendously in loosening up the white people and bridging racial divisions.

Another challenge for us white people was swaying to the rhythm of the music. It wasn't unusual for some of us to be swaying in wrong direction. We literally had to designate Joe as the *"sway meister."* When we would begin a song, all of my white sisters and brothers would focus on the sway meister.

These were some of the unseen challenges we faced as we broke racial and religious barriers. The joy of breaking racial barriers in the deep South and the solidarity we co-created was profoundly satisfying to my Soul.

THE CANARY IN THE COAL MINE

In my opinion, multiple sclerosis is a catchall for different disorders. Medical science is in the dark ages when it comes to finding the etiology and then effective treatments for autoimmune illnesses.

There are many imbalances in our culture that lead to even greater imbalances. The ravages of aggression over love is probably the greatest imbalance which needs to be addressed for greater wellness in our world.

I believe that imbalances on the 'psychospiritual level' create disorder on the more dense levels. A valid and personal example is becoming more evident on the microbial level. I became aware that microbes and stealth infections were on the rise when I was diagnosed with Lyme disease in 2004 and underwent treatment. An eye-opening documentary titled, *Under Our Skin* received critical acclaim for describing the imbalances that are accelerating and threatening many individuals. (The documentary can be ordered free of charge on the Internet.)

I was treated for a number of years by a world renowned Lyme disease specialist noted in the documentary previously mentioned. Sitting in his office in Seattle, other healthcare professionals and I discussed how many of his patients struggled with multiple illnesses including multiple sclerosis, autism and others - they were the *canaries in the coal mines.* Our culture and our lifestyle choices have elicited a proliferation of imbalances causing infections and immune systems that are insufficient for keeping these microbes in balance.

Many of the friends I have met with serious injuries and illnesses are coming into greater balance with their challenges, their body's are healing. I believe if people consciously choose to address their lifestyle choices and work through their emotional issues, this will bring them into greater wholeness and into a state of *love*, love of self and others. With less struggle in the world, there will be more joy...*That has been my Sacred Path.*

Just opening to the possibility of the bigger picture perspective for healing raises the vibration of each of us, for us and our loved ones.

CHAPTER NINE
I WILL MEET YOU BY THE RIVER

"Bringing something to share with others... something with the power to heal a wounded land..." Joseph Campbell

ILLNESS: A TRANSPERSONAL PERSPECTIVE

Blog Entry: July 29, 2014

"When you become a lover of what is, the war is over."- Byron Katie

As recorded in these blogs, I have engaged in many kinds of healing therapies over the years: both conventional and unconventional psychotherapy, Holotropic breathwork, energy work, 'stem cell' and many others. All of of these therapies have helped me in different ways, including the understanding of the significance of this illness in my life. To open even further the perspective of my soul's trajectory, I've done another therapy which I mentioned briefly before, called 'hypnotherapy.'

The reason I engaged this therapy was to more fully explore the possibility that this illness possibly occurred...*to initiate my highest evolution.* I understand that many people do not believe in reincarnation and the concept of 'past lives' is foreign to them, so it is acceptable to me to use the term 'symbolic story.'

As in dreams, the symbolism one experiences during hypnosis is never arbitrary. Through hypnosis, I was able to explore a past life, or symbolic story, where I was in Eastern Europe during the 40s. I was a wealthy Jewish woman who clung to her material items and was thrown into the street with all my neighbors *like cattle.* Later, I experienced my last thoughts as I died in a gas chamber and I thought about how, during this life...*I realized that I was not my material things.*

Then, like a time-life documentary we fast-forward to the time just before my present lifetime begins and I am exploring my choices for this lifetime.

I see that I've chosen the possibility of catastrophic illness and that this choice could direct me to my highest purpose. This purpose being that I would learn *that I am not my body.* I would learn, by experience, that the body is merely a vehicle that is chosen and used for the lifetime and then dies and that I chose a strong, beautiful and dependable body to support me in this journey. This evolution would surprise people and shock them, perhaps...*into realizing their own evolutions.*

All of this confirmed my earlier insights, although at the time of these therapeutic experiences I was still far from seeing this tremendous challenge as being something positive. Since my life has always been about transformation and service, it gave me joy to feel like I might be doing my part to forward the evolution of the planet and its many people.

The constellation of my life has changed tremendously since my diagnosis. Many friends have moved away from me, some at lightning speed. I have compassion for them because my circumstances can elicit the fear..."*if that happened to her, it could happen to me or my loved ones.*" I can remember feeling that way myself about frightening circumstances. The people in my life, however, who *could* hold my experience *grew exponentially.*. Actually, I'd like to see that everyone has grown from this, even those who left, because seeing your limitations can be transformative in and of itself.

Accepting the comings *and goings* has been a large part of letting go of will and moving toward acceptance. Through acceptance I have felt liberated and moved into a state of joy and deep connection. Inner and outer connectedness is the likely outcome when one has the spiritual maturity to *stay*. The Tibetan nun, Pema Chodrun, teaches a practice of *staying*, as in staying in the chaos of transformational change. When I saw that I could find joy in these circumstances, I knew I could find joy in any. After all, who gets to unpack and consider every aspect of their life one event at a time?

This week was spent going through all of my clothing and jewelry, *choosing their destinations:* this is for Casey, this is for Jordan, this goes to the Free Box in Crestone and so on. I am concurrently grieving and celebrating every aspect of my life over a sixty year span. Also this week, I completed my end of life paperwork which will enable me to have an open air cremation that is legal in Crestone. When the time comes, whether it be in ten years or ten minutes, I have created my closing act down to the Native American flute and Taiko drums. I get to do that.

This process has not been easy. On the contrary, it has been fraught with much grief, thoughtfulness and life review. *What have I left incomplete? What relationships are less than clean and loving?* I can even project into the future, to anticipate future needs of my children and grandchildren and communicate with them...*like time travel.* Casey set up e-mail addresses for her boys and I'll date the messages such that they'll have future communication from me!

How fortunate I feel to be able to be present with myself and with my children through this process. Really...*who gets to do this?*

Arroyo Secco, New Mexico - 1999

TRIANGLES: THE POWER OF THREE

Blog Entry: August 4, 2014

"Should you shield the canyons from the windstorms, you would never see the beauty in their carvings." – Elisabeth Kubler-Ross

When I was a child there was a rule of thumb, rarely would you have two girls visit if you could at all avoid it. That could be a recipe for disaster...*three girls together!*

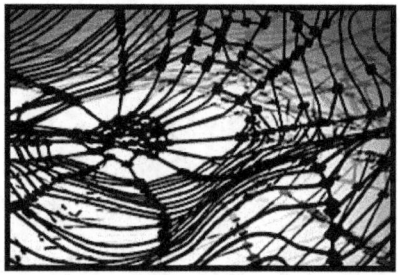

I don't know what it was about three, but it surely could elicit conflict.

I wonder if it is specific to our culture or if it is a human characteristic. Triangles surely offer an evocative relationship dynamic. In relationship theory, there is a term called triangulation where a couple draws in a third person to relieve anxiety in the original dyad. Anxiety is usually a symptom of tension, a kind of tension which builds because the couple needs to undergo change to attain greater authenticity. Confronting this dynamic creates even greater levels of tension and it takes much integrity and spiritual development to make the necessary shift. This is the high road perhaps but nevertheless, the power of these triangles can challenge people to reach a higher level of authenticity.

Another manifestation of triangles is when the energy of two forces becomes polarized. As the two forces move toward changing to a greater equilibrium, the polarization escalates. When a mediating third force enters the field, transformation can happen. The art of *mediation* is an example of this process.

When I went to the Grof Transpersonal Training I met many wonderful people who became my sacred community for three years. Two of the people would help me to connect the dots from significant relationship traumas, which led to my deepest relational healing.

In order to fully communicate the level of healing this represented, I need to describe the circumstances that ended my second marriage. This marriage held both a great deal of love and an equal amount of childhood trauma. Although we worked tenaciously to heal the trauma, the wounds were too great and we were losing ground. My neurological symptoms had become evident and were slowly progressing. Intuitively I knew that if the circumstances didn't change, I could die. All life choices were made from this perspective at this point in my life, extreme as it may sound. Unfortunately, at the time I didn't understand the level of pressure I was under, nor did I know how to relieve it.

Part of our attempt to heal childhood trauma brought us to Galisteo, New Mexico to work with a healer named Rick. Rick and I made a deep connection which was destabilizing for me for my marriage. I attempted to work with his wife, but found her to be emotionally distant. Suffice it to say that I was not developed enough to deal with the tension in my relationship. Drama ensued and my marriage ended in a devastating way, with much betrayal and shame.

Now back to the transpersonal training I mentioned above and the two people who helped me so much. I will call the couple X and Y to preserve their privacy.

My original connection with X was, at the beginning of this training, as my massage therapist - a relationship which I found very *grounding* for my ensuing journey. Little did I know how auspicious this would be in healing my most primal trauma. Her husband, Y and I connected deeply as well. We became breathwork partners for most of the modules during the next three years.

One auspicious day, I entered the training module, late which was unusual for me. I claimed the only seat left in the large room, which happened to be between and slightly behind the two of them. While I sat there this overwhelming wave of emotion overcame me. Sitting in a triangle with the two of them brought up my trauma from the New Mexico couple. Unwilling to repeat a scenario which brought so much pain, I asked X to talk with me. I told her the whole story of the last triangle and the pain it brought to all concerned. Contrary to what I expected, she was enormously empathetic and acknowledged my *pain*, something I had not acknowledged through the shame. In her wisdom, she *got* the significance of the devastation. Her empathy in the moment provided the alchemical heat needed...*to transform lead into gold.*

It was due to my honesty and her love that I was able to clear the shame I had been carrying all these years. This validated my belief that the only true elixir is love. I was able to understand the primal trauma that was being healed...*the triangle with my parents.*

My mother, with her wounding from childhood, was unable to offer me the love and nurturance I needed. Unconsciously, I had wanted to heal this pathological pattern with Rick's wife. When she was emotionally unavailable, the old pattern kicked in exaggerating the importance of the man - a pattern I had unconsciously played out over and over in my relationships. When X offered love and empathy, she metaphorically offered to hold the kite string. Despite knowing my history, she trusted me. These leaps of faith require courage and a commitment to love and her generosity allowed for significant relational healing in my life.

To reference the late Maya Angelou once again, *"when someone knows better, they do better."* Sometimes, knowing better can require everything from you, but the alternative of living unconsciously is much more painful.

Y continues to be my doctor to this day. They came together to deliver supplements yesterday and I thanked them once again for their wisdom and their love. With tears in our eyes, we acknowledged the healing power of *this* triangle.

RIVER AND LUC

Blog Entry: August 11, 2014

"When you do things from your soul, you feel a river in you, a joy."
– Rumi

Without my two grand boys, I would not be a grandmother. I cannot write a blog of love and regeneration and not include my beautiful boys River and Luc!

River was born in 2011, in Brooklyn when I briefly lived nearby. We drove two hours to the hospital in New York City and I saw him when he was a few hours old. Luc was born exactly two years later and in a mysterious and unseen way, despite being far away in Colorado this time...*I felt as if I were present* and experiencing the blessed event with my children. What an amazing feeling to see our families meld into one little being with so much promise!

I wondered what sort of grandmother I might be, confined to a wheelchair and with so much disability. I had always imagined myself throwing them in the air and 'flying them', with their stomachs against my feet like I did with my children. What sort of grandmother could I be to my grandchildren?

One day, when Casey was pregnant, I posed that question to them at a vulnerable moment. Feeling that I might be relapsing into the belief that I am my physicality, my son-in-law broke through my mood with, *"It's like, you offer a register of consciousness."* An electric shock wave sped through me and I was reminded of who I truly am...*and what my Sacred mission is* even here and now, with them.

So, *my beloved River and Luc,* I will not be sitting on the floor with you, I will not be holding books to read with you but I will hold...*a frequency of Love* and I will follow your lives wherever they will take you. I will be in the wind if you listen closely. I will be in the water tickling you and I will be in the sun's rays warming your skin. You can learn to listen closely and you will hear my words of love and encouragement. You will never be without me in your hearts and that will be true for any other siblings or cousins in the future.

My life has brought many surprises to me and to others and this has provided many opportunities for...*deepening.* I hope that we can *all* meet together...*in that field of Love and Depth.*

CAREGIVING: TRANSCENDING DUALITY

Blog Entry: August 18, 2014

"Love motivates service, and service gives form to love." – Robert Schwartz

There is something that happens during a caregiving scenario, when the level of disability is so extreme that the caregiver needs total focus for keeping the individual's life from being in jeopardy. This is the quality that develops between myself and my caregivers.

The level of disability I experience is profound. I cannot move a limb to avoid a potential catastrophe. My caregiver is vitally important for the most basic skills.

Fortunately, only a small percentage of people with multiple sclerosis ever experience this level of disability. I have come to believe that the degree of disability is not arbitrary but it is commensurate with what is required for a necessary outcome...*the evolution of one's higher purpose.*

This understanding is not held by the majority of people, but I believe it is a necessary understanding when one accepts that *the universe is perfectly safe.* To accept this premise one must subscribe to love over fear and to arrive at the state of *Love*, I've needed to move through much fear.

As they say, *"the only way is through"* and this was surely true for me. Surrendering to this illness was a way for me to learn to accept being cared for on many levels.

Something magical can happen during caregiving when a certain level of *oneness* is achieved through this intense level of focus. The potential for this to occur became clear while being bathed in my outdoor shower. Allison is my caregiver for this blissful endeavor and we have been working together for over two years.

The level of focus required to keep me safe is not a minimal feat. There is the transfer to the shower chair, the slippery soap and the flying insects during the Colorado summer. Yes, we have an inundation of mosquitoes, gnats, noseeums, horseflies and any other bug you can imagine. My alkaline diet seems to provide a deterrent for the little ones, but not for the more aggressive types!

Contrary to popular understanding about multiple sclerosis, my body is not numb. When there is a fly walking across my skin I feel every sensation. When a mosquito stings me, I feel the intrusion. Actually, my bodily sensation is to a degree...*heightened*. When I felt the horsefly on my leg, without hesitation Allison swatted the bug full force. Allison was surprised that she didn't feel the sting in her own thigh. That is how heightened the caregiving symbiosis can become. It can be a curriculum of transcendence...*or oneness.*

Once I was able to go beyond the profound fear of the illness and to understand the bigger picture rather than feeling victimized by the loss of body functioning, I was able to open to relationships where I could receive care on some of the deepest levels.

My ego would never have chosen this degree of vulnerability and from the ego's perspective these circumstances are a tragedy. From the bigger picture perspective, I am learning...*unitive consciousness* or *Oneness* on many levels. Loving interactions with my caregivers are some of the more significant teachings...*for which I am tremendously grateful.*

The waxing and waning of emotion
Collects in a convulsion
Releasing
Cleansing

And if I die before I wake
pray the Lord my soul to take
And when I finally make it through
The collective will smile
With gifts deep and lasting
And my Home will be renewed

I WOULDN'T WANT TO BE A MEMBER OF A GROUP THAT WOULD HAVE ME AS A MEMBER - Groucho Marx

Blog Entry: August 28, 2014

I am calling hospice today to see if I qualify for their services. There are few services available to those living in the wilderness, even the home health organization cannot provide outreach for our area anymore. Although I am self-sufficient, occasionally there are issues that are beyond me medically.

For example, a few weeks ago my heart rate went to 152 while I was standing and I didn't know who to consult.

The decision to call hospice comes from me. Nobody referred me to them, not the home health organization that regretfully discharge me, my primary care doctor, nor my caregivers or friends - some of whom are nurses. I don't think anyone wanted to connect me with *that* organization. So it wasn't a matter of neglect or oversight, but perhaps it was more a matter of denial...*and grief.*

We called and although I don't qualify for their short-term program *(hooray!),* I do qualify for their long-term palliative care program. Palliative care is defined as a multidisciplinary approach to providing medical care for those with serious illnesses to relieve pain, symptoms and stress. The administrative person explained the program and said that with a doctor's order I could sign the paperwork. I explained that I cannot use my hands and she suggested a power of attorney. A power of attorney to me suggests deferring power to another. Doesn't she realize that is what I have done my whole life?! I refuse to do it now. My suggestion was duct tape, but she didn't seem to appreciate that.

There is a part of me, by the way, who is in charge much of the time...*that really does not take this seriously.* When you have a life-threatening illness for as long as I have and have moved through acceptance to a state of transcendence, it is hard to take these circumstances too seriously...*I would be way too serious, way too often!* I had to give that up.

I feel like someone who is about to go on a beautiful journey and is excited about the adventure. Thinking about one's place of departure is not really the point when you are going on a *'pilgrimage'*. There is much I'll be glad to not have to deal with, like my in-floor radiant heat, the physical discomfort I deal with on a daily basis and the enormous energy it takes...*just to stay alive.* When I think of my greatest grief, it is in leaving my children and grandchildren, but as I open more to the belief that I will not be truly leaving them, what's the point? It's not like I can go skiing, swimming or riding anymore. After all, once we all make our transitions...*we will be together again.*

So, while I may have the dubious distinction of soon being in a group in which I do not desire membership. I am a member of a broader group, a group formed and expressed through *Love* and...*I embrace that membership!*

I WILL MEET YOU BY THE RIVER

"Out beyond ideas of wrongdoing and right doing, there is a field. I'll meet you there!" - Rumi

I was just watching *The Piano*, a 1990 film set in mid-19th-century New Zealand and I had a complete shift in consciousness. I had been feeling a deep level of despair for more than twenty-four hours.

My bouts with despair have decreased appreciably over the years...*but this was a big one.* I was immersed in the multiple losses I have been experiencing over many years. My story of loss is compelling given the crescendo of circumstances. I don't need to list them, they are pretty obvious...*but the affect can be tremendously dispiriting.*

If you've seen and remember the film, a piano falls overboard with the rope around Holly Hunter's ankle, it is an iconic moment that most people can recall. What I didn't remember is that she freed herself and, as she struggled for breath, swam to the surface. She survived! She freed herself from the weight of the piano that had been both her salvation and her destroyer. In that moment, my perceptions shifted. Instead of seeing the litany of losses, I realized I had...*let them go.* I revisited each significant loss and saw that I had let it go. I was no longer oppressed by my perception. I felt the courage it had taken...*I felt empowered.*

This is how tragedy has moved into transcendence one moment at a time over the twenty years of this profound curriculum. I have so much gratitude for the teachings, gratitude for my perseverance, gratitude for the support from my family and friends and, yes...*even gratitude for the illness*. The persistent depression I experienced in my early years has shifted to great joy and expansiveness. My relationships with people have deepened considerably in general and with my children, *profoundly*. My ability to contribute to others and to touch more lives has grown exponentially through this illness.

My acceptance of impermanence has led to knowing what is truly permanent...*and that is Love*. I know that I will never lose anything that is grounded in love. I will not lose my children, I will not lose my grandchildren. In truth, as I have been able to *listen* more deeply, my parents, who are now deceased, are more available to me emotionally than ever they were in life.

I have learned and integrated that this is a loving and safe Universe. I have learned this from the inside out.

"Out beyond ideas of wrongdoing and right doing, there is a field. I'll meet you there!" - Rumi

With these teachings I know that I will meet my loved ones in that field that Rumi writes of,

I will meet you by the river.

FINAL MEDITATION - *September 21, 2014*

"Our true home is in the present moment. The miracle is not to walk on water. The miracle is to walk on the green earth in the present moment." Thich Nhat Hanh

I've been a human 'doing' most of my life. It seems to have been by *subtraction* that I found out who I truly was. This process of eliminating levels and levels of identity was excruciating and it was only by releasing these identities that I found out how enslaved I was. Life threatening illness was my greatest teacher in learning to *be* in the present moment.

Ironically, entering a process with life-threatening illness has afforded me my most Spiritual experience. I've had the opportunity to *sit* and focus on my internal world, a world that yearned for completion with relationships and preparation for my loved ones.

I have been given the opportunity to bask in expansive feelings of love and interconnectedness.

And I have realized my deepest passion...*to become a clearer vessel for helping myself and others.* **Thank you for joining me in my journey...**

I hope my journey helps you in yours.

- Aliyah

UPDATE
STILL HERE: RAM DASS

Blog Entry: September 24, 2014

I'm stealing your title, Baba! I'm upright in my standing frame and in my beautiful courtyard pictured below and I want to offer an update.

The hospice nurse visited, because I felt like I needed more medical support and, being so remote, the home health organization could not secure a nurse to drive this far.

As I described my sense of isolation to the nurse, I shed a tiny tear. The isolation is not geographic, it is not even a social description, it is the feeling one has when moving toward an unknown, and maybe toward...*the Great Unknown.* In spite of my energy level, the nurse began to fit me into the six-month program. Her requirement was that I give up physical therapy. When I saw the direction this trajectory was taking, I realized that I'm at a crossroads. *Am I willing to give up my regenerative life?*

I clearly could see either possibility and could visit each without judgment.

I saw that my inner being was not ready to let go of my protocols. This could change tomorrow, but for now I still have 'places' to go and people to see! My naturopathic doctor's wife reasons that, *"people will want to interact with me after the book is out."*

Interestingly enough, once I made this decision, I got an e-mail from the home health organization who hired a nurse from Crestone. That is kind of how it rolls when we are aware of life's synchronicities.

So for now I will be 'standing' in my courtyard every morning, riding my stationary bike...*and writing.*

And who knows what tomorrow will bring!

You may reach Aliyah at www.meetmebytheriver.net

ABOUT THE AUTHOR

Aliyah Alexander earned her BA degree in psychology from the University of Miami, and her MSW from The Tulane School of Social Work. She is an accredited Grof Transpersonal Trainer and breathwork facilitator and has maintained a Private Practice in psychotherapist for twenty years.

Aliyah raised her children in the New Orleans area and moved to Crestone, Colorado after hurricane Katrina. She lives there with her cat Pikachu at the foot of 14,000 foot mountains. She meditates, thinks about her life and how telling her remarkable story can be of service to others.

This book was created from blogs, journals and poems which she has kept and written over the years of Alyah's life. You can visit the blog at aliyahonline.wordpress.com.

FURTHER CLARIFICATION

I have always been a person who pushed my own boundaries into areas where growth was assured. As a professional, I have pushed others' boundaries past their comfort zones as well. I used to say in my groups that if you don't want to quit at one point or another, the group is not good enough. Left to our own devices...*we will stay in our comfort zones.*

It is equally important for each person to check inside themselves to see what resonates as Truth for them. Many of my concepts and beliefs are not necessarily universal. These have become my particular beliefs over a very long period of time. At different points I would have argued vociferously about many of my beliefs. I welcome differing views.

I also want to mention a certain disclaimer that 'choosing' one's illness or injury is not done with the mind. Some people believe that they are being punished by physical illness or injury. This couldn't be further from the truth. Early in the process I believed that and only after I began healing my shame and guilt, did I begin to open up to greater possibilities. I, my ego, would never have chosen multiple sclerosis, a catastrophic disability where I could be a burden to others. If I believed that my ego or personality chose this, I could feel my shame. That is not the purpose of this understanding. The concept is profoundly empowering, if one is able to open up to the possibility that one's *higher self* 'chose' this curriculum for one's *highest good.*

I believe we work in concert with our spirit guides to make these choices. It has taken me a long time to subscribe to this understanding. And for many, I understand that it is a stretch. It would have been for me a few years ago.

So, if some of my concepts are disturbing just hang in there and understand that we all have different beliefs and philosophies. What I ask myself is, if this were true...*do I feel more empowered or disempowered?* My work has always been about *self* empowerment and *other* empowerment.

So thank you for coming on this journey with me! I hope it is thought-provoking and evocative.

Much love,
- Aliyah

ORIGIN OF TITLE

The title of this book comes from my daughter Casey. She'd read the entry River and Luc and remembered our home on the Tchefuncte River in Louisiana where children played, had birthday parties and explored. Casey wrote:

"I've been thinking about where I will find you, when you are no longer physically you. I've been thinking about making something, maybe photographs, or a film, or something about the speckled light rays and wind in the sounds of nature. I'm not sure how it will take form or when I will make it, but the visuals I'm imagining are in our backyard and the title is "I'll Meet You By The River."

Aliyah's friends and caregivers write ,

Aliyah writes this blog from a very particular and beautiful spot on this planet. She dwells in Crestone, a remote town in southern Colorado, nestled in the foothills of the Sangre de Cristo Mountains. The fourteen thousand foot peaks give way to a wide expanse - a high valley at eight thousand feet which many native and hispanic peoples have traversed for centuries. The silence there is exquisite, the sky very blue and the landscape appeals to the deeper parts of one's being.

Within this vast expanse, Aliyah is physically confined to a large circular space in her home. She has a degenerative disease which causes her immobility of body, but in her words...*she lives a regenerative life.*

She lives her life wide open, no buffers, no confidentiality. She dedicates her life force to nurturing people into the fuller, deeper aspects of themselves and of their lives. She has a network of care partners and physical therapists who have helped her live with independence and dignity. She supports them with a triweekly circle, to facilitate the cohesion and to allow all around her to share their hearts openly, in safety and non-judgment.

In this way she lives a new vision of healing, one where our 'curriculums' are our steppingstones and our common ground to grow and expand a more loving world.

– Judith Oakland and Kathryn Brady

www.ingramcontent.com/pod-product-compliance
Lightning Source LLC
Chambersburg PA
CBHW050628300426
44112CB00012B/1709